Love Letters

The Romantic Secrets Hidden in Our Handwriting

by

Paula Roberts

New Page Books
a Division of The Career Press, Inc.
Franklin Lakes, NJ

LOVE LETTERS
Edited by Kristen Mohn
Typeset by John J. O'Sullivan
Cover design by Cheryl Cohan Finbow
Printed in the U.S.A. by Book-mart Press

To order this title, please call toll-free 1-800-CAREER-1 (NJ and Canada: 201-848-0310) to order using VISA or MasterCard, or for further information on books from Career Press.

The Career Press, Inc.,
3 Tice Road, PO Box 687, Franklin Lakes, NJ 07417
www.careerpress.com
www.newpagebooks.com

Library of Congress Cataloging-in-Publication Data

Roberts, Paula.

Love letters: the romantic secrets hidden in our handwriting / by Paula Roberts.

    p. cm.

Includes bibliographical references and index.

    ISBN 1-56414-587-5

    1. Graphology. 2. Love--Miscellanea. 3. Interpersonal relations--Miscellanea. I. Title.

BF905.L68 R63 2002

155.2'82--dc21   2001044362

Dedication

This book is dedicated to the memory of
Leslie "Johnny"Roberts,
whose writing provided the ultimate challenge to read.
Also to our mother,
Joyce Melton
who always inspired us to
take on new ventures.

Acknowledgments

My first debt of thanks must go to Patricia Marne with whom I studied graphology in London back in 1974. It was her inspired teaching and enthusiasm for her subject that led to my fascination with handwriting analysis.

I must also thank the very many friends who, over the years, have given me literally hundreds of samples of the writings of interesting people, both famous and unknown. These have proved to be invaluable in putting this book together. (The samples used here are to illustrate certain personality traits, without any personal criticism implied or intended.)

A particular thank you to Pete Siegal and Bob Schagrin of GOTTA HAVE IT!, 153 East 57th Street, New York City 10021 (also of London) for allowing me to use the following samples: Houdini, John Lennon, Jayne Mansfield, Mick Jagger, Joe Namath, Ernest Hemingway, Babe Ruth, Bruce Springsteen, Madonna, Sir Arthur Conan Doyle, George Gershwin, Erte, President Kennedy, Stevie Nicks, Boris Karloff, and Kurt Cobain.

Many thanks go to Ingo Swann, curator of the Cosmic Art archives and correspondence of Raymond F. Piper and Lila K. Piper, for the following samples: Georgia O'Keefe, Rockwell Kent, C.G. Jung, Barbara Hepworth, Mark Rothko, and Dane Rhudyar.

Linda Mason very kindly photographed many of these samples for me, for which I thank her. Also Eric Pederson used his drawing skills to illustrate some of the doodles, for which I am most grateful.

A final and very special thank you to my agent, Lisa Hagan of Paraview, who always had faith in this book.

Contents

Introduction

Wouldn't it be a wonderful advantage in life if you could find a way to quickly discover which people you are compatible with just by looking at a small piece of their handwriting? In today's fast-paced world, the luxury of writing long personal letters seems to have been largely replaced by telephone calls and e-mail. Even so, everyone still does write from time to time, and it is the day-to-day notes, letters, and jottings that can give you enormous insight into a person's character.

Perhaps you have never realized that each time you put pen to paper, you are leaving a description of yourself far more revealing than you could possibly imagine. Each person's signature is as unique as his or her fingerprints or DNA. That is why it is legally binding.

How many of us have an old love letter or two tucked away in a secret place? Many times this letter was written by someone we hardly ever think of now, yet we are still reluctant to throw away this most personal of possessions. In a way, it reminds us of how very highly we were thought of at some time in the past. Now, the written word has become much more valued than the writer. I do not think that we will live to cherish an e-mail in this same way.

Graphology, as handwriting analysis is termed, is not a passing fad. There is nothing occult, New

Age, or mysterious about it. Lying somewhere between art and science, it has a long and respectable history starting as far back as the ancient Romans. The historian Suetonius Tranquillus was among the first to notice in the writings of several emperors he was researching that the letters were formed differently in each case. He theorized that this could indicate different character traits. In their 17th-century writing, Alerius Prosper and Camilla Baldo also suggested that you could make connections between different handwritings and personalities. The 19th-century work by Abbott Jean-Hippolyte Michon and Abbott Flandrin, in which they collected innumerable handwriting samples and matched styles of writing with various temperaments, was the beginning of modern graphology. Indeed, it was Abbott Michon who coined the term "graphology."

Today, graphology is used extensively worldwide by businesses and institutions such as the FBI and the CIA. Even the U.S. Supreme Court has taken it seriously enough to rule that because handwriting is viewed by the public, analysis of it is not an invasion of privacy. If they find it reliable enough to use for character analysis, then perhaps you may want to employ it in making one of the most important decisions in your life: who to spend it with.

In the pages that follow, you will find useful and easy-to-understand information, using only small samples of handwriting, that will help you make better choices of romantic partners. Organized according to a particular character trait, each chapter of this book focuses on a specific principle and offers concise explanations. The aim is not to turn you into a professional graphologist, but rather to enable you to learn enough about your partner's personality to gauge the possibility of success in the relationship. This book may also cause you to reflect as much on your own characteristics as on those of your partner.

Graphology is a remarkably effective way of peering into the subconscious responses to all areas of life, which is why, in the past, it has been called "brain-writing." Strangely enough, it even works perfectly well when someone who invariably prints is asked to use script (which is essential for analysis). No one seems to know quite why it works, but it does.

To start, you need a handwriting sample written with pencil on unlined paper. The sample should contain the following words: "I live in New York City and my name is…" (which is followed underneath by the person's regular signature). This is a perfect combination of words with a variety of upper and lower loops, capital letters, and lowercase letters. It is not an homage to the city I have made my home since 1978, but it is easier to write than the traditional "The quick brown fox jumped over the lazy dog."

Obviously, it is not always possible to get someone to write something specifically for you to analyze. Don't worry—rest assured that a few words scribbled on a birthday card or a notepad is often enough to make a start. What is essential is that the sample must be written in script, never printed.

For many years I have started each session with a new client by first looking at their own handwriting, followed by any other samples they may have brought with them. As I always demand to know nothing about my clients prior to the first meeting, everything about the strengths, weaknesses, and quirks of their character is learned entirely through the handwriting analysis. It is in this way that I have exhaustively tested the rules of compatibility in relationships. After a period of experimentation, you may find, as I did years ago, that you will trust your handwriting analysis of a person more than most other forms of character assessment.

One final word: there is nothing in handwriting that can tell you whether two people are going to love each other and wish to work out a relationship despite all the obstacles. Love is a mystery to us all, but handwriting is a great help in seeing what those obstacles and opportunities may be.

Chapter 1

Introvert
or Extrovert?

Suzy* and the personals

S uzy had been having problems finding the right man. She had patiently gone on all the blind dates that kind friends (and interfering relatives) had set up for her—but so far, they were without any success. By the time she came to me, Suzy was already somewhat despairing about her chances for love.

When clients come to see me, they usually bring just one or two samples of handwriting for me to analyze. To my great surprise, Suzy pulled dozens of envelopes out of her bag. She explained to me that her roommate had talked her into putting an ad in the personals and that these were all of the responses. She was overwhelmed by the thought of trying to pick someone out of such a large number and was wondering if handwriting analysis could be of any assistance. I assured her that it certainly could!

Suzy worked in a health club as a personal trainer, so she met plenty of people in the course of her work. Her manner was pleasant and outgoing and

*All names have been changed to protect the privacy of the clients involved.

she was also pretty and well-groomed. Despite this, she was beginning to think that perhaps there was something wrong with her or that she was just being too picky. Neither was true. She was not looking for a mythical Mr. Perfect, just Mr. All Right for love, companionship, and a feeling of working together in a partnership for life.

I always like a challenge, so I took all of the letters out of their envelopes (incidentally, envelopes are not good samples for analysis as people tend to make them more legible and tidy than their natural writing might be). Then I spread them out over a large table. Puzzled, Suzy asked, "How can you read them like that?" "I am not going to actually read them, I never do," I replied. In looking for characteristics it is not necessary to read the content of a letter, and sometimes it only adds confusion. What I was looking for were personality traits that matched hers. I was not interested in reading what someone thought were his most impressive attributes. I was looking for the truth about the man.

Reflecting her outgoing personality, Suzy's writing sloped to the right, which indicates a sociable, team-oriented kind of person. Knowing Suzy's personality, I put all the candidates' writings that sloped off to the left or were straight up and down to one side. These belonged to introverted or very independent people and there would be no reason to try to match her with people who had very different social needs. That still left us with about a dozen people.

Next I picked out four letters that had not only the right-hand slope, but were also written with very wide letters and curved letter endings. These traits would denote a good match with her generous and warm personality. She was understandably nervous and asked if I was sure about these men. I truthfully explained that no one can be entirely sure that two people will actually take a liking to each other, but I did know that these men shared a lot in common with her as far as being open and sociable. The rest would be up to her.

Several months later, she asked me if I would perform her wedding service the following summer as one of my "picks" had worked out perfectly. I was a little tempted during the service to give credit to the powers of handwriting for this happy union, but decided that the origins of their relationship would remain our little secret.

The 1st Secret for Finding Your Perfect Match:

Slant

As with most things in life, there is a place to begin when looking at someone's handwriting. That place is the direction in which the writing slants—to the right, the left, or straight up and down. The slant will give you an idea of how much (or how little) a person is drawn toward other people. Interestingly enough, it makes no difference whether the person is right- or left-handed.

Are you looking for a blend of energies and attitudes similar to your own that would create a high comfort level? The traditional rules of handwriting analysis (and of romance) say that this is what you must look for in a long-lasting relationship. These rules tend to overlook the fact that some people thrive on conflict and to them, such a harmonious situation spells death brought on by boredom. Again, this book may cause you to reflect just as much on yourself as on the other person, for we cannot change anyone else. The question you must ask yourself is: Can you accept the way your partner is? When we understand ourselves, we are much better equipped to find a suitable partner.

When you are looking for someone with a similar personality to your own, check to see if the slope of your partner's writing matches yours. It is easy to see with the naked eye if the slope is somewhat the same, but to be more precise, draw a straight line under the writing. Then see if your partner's and your own writing are nearly in the same slope.

It is necessary to understand that even when the slopes are exactly the same, this does not automatically guarantee a happy life together. Rather, it indicates that you both enjoy the same degree of interaction with the rest of the world. It is a very important sign of compatibility, but it is not the only one. If you are looking for the excitement of a turbulent relationship, you may want to find someone whose writing slopes in a different way than your own.

About three-quarters of the population's writing does have some degree of slant to the right showing, quite literally, a movement toward people and the person to whom the letter is being written. The right-hand slant has always been understood to signify an extroverted personality—more interested in the environment and other people than in self. This is not necessarily always accurate. It might be better to suggest that these people have an emotional response to the world. They are affected by the opinions and actions of others, which is not the same as being friendly by nature, although they do tend to need people available to them with whom they can share their ideas and experiences. Left entirely by themselves, they do not tend to do too well.

In general terms, the right slant tends to show us a person who is a team player or supportive in character. Elizabeth Taylor's example (page 14), which is represented smaller than it's actual size, has a slope which clearly indicates someone who has a

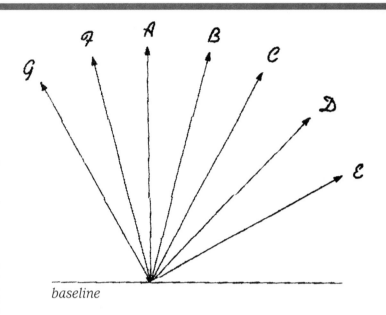

baseline

Place the writing on the baseline and see which direction the upper loops slant.

A **Independent:** a person who happily goes about his business without seeking the approval of others.

B-C **Middle emotional range:** the majority of people who enjoy the support and companionship of friends, family, and colleagues.

C-D **Easily influenced:** these people are frequently swayed by the moods of others (not always to their benefit).

D-E **Extreme reactions:** these people are repeatedly out of control of their own lives and excessively affected by those around them.

A-F **Analytical:** people who deal in a cool manner, using their heads before their emotions; not unfriendly, but cautious.

F-G **Withdrawn:** these few people are intensely private and often reclusive in nature; mistrustful of others.

Elizabeth Taylor

Thank you for making my day so special.

Love,
Elizabeth

This fiery, emotional actress's writing is almost exactly on the "C" slope, right where we would expect it.

great need of relationships, as her multiple marriages suggest. When you see that writing has an extreme slant to the right (almost falling on it's face), the writer should, in fact, be viewed with some caution because it indicates a person whose emotions may be out of control; at the least, these are people who can be very excitable. Barbra Streisand's writing below shows a very right-hand slope and it is said by those who know her well that she is a rather temperamental person.

Barbra Streisand

I have this painting on reverse - It supposedly is a painting of high quality - in excellent condition - The price

Barb

The slope of this writing is on the "D" line showing her to be extremely emotionally driven as befits a successful diva.

The straight-backed, up-and-down writing of the independent person indicates someone more comfortable making up their own mind about issues and neither asking, nor welcoming much advice. This does not mean that they are purely stubborn, they are just someone who can stand on their own (and tends to wish others would as well). Initially, these writers can be seen as poised and reserved, and indeed they do take time before they make a commitment. These people can also make wonderful partners if their loved ones are able to give them a certain amount of

---

George Gershwin

SHIP TO *GEORGE GERSHWIN 132 EAST 72nd STREET NEW YORK CITY*

SIGNED: *George Gershwin*

It is understood the final right to be sold in New York sometime in May 1935 is to be mine. G.G.

This brilliant musician's writing goes straight up and down which clearly shows that he followed his own beat.

---

space and freedom. Sometimes their apparent need to control, in fact, masks deep insecurity. People as diverse as George Gershwin (above) and Margaret Thatcher (page 16) both have this very independent writing.

The left (leaning backwards) slant was called introverted, but this term does not create a complete picture. Analytical is a much better description of these people who tend to be led by head before heart. Many times they are rather self-conscious and shy when surrounded by company, feeling somewhat isolated. In apparent complete contrast, they can sometimes seem positively flamboyant for short periods of time. They think things through rather than reacting on a gut feeling.

It would be a mistake to believe that these people are anti-social because many of them lead very socially active lives.

What they do need, though, is quite a lot of time and space to regroup themselves, as they tend to become overwhelmed by too much contact with others. They do not appreciate (nor need) someone asking them how they are every five minutes. Although about two-thirds of the population does

Margaret Thatcher

impossible J Jean.
It was very nice of you to think of asking me –
with my warmest thanks – regrets.
Yours very sincerely
Margaret

The "Iron Lady's" writing is clearly straight up and down on the "A" slope. Anyone who knows anything about the former prime minister would surely agree that she is not a person to be unduly influenced by others.

have writing that slopes to the right, which indicates greater cooperation with others, not everyone has to be a team person. Think how boring the world would be if every one of us was the same. There is nothing *wrong* in not being mainstream. They are at their happiest being allowed to set their own pace regarding the amount of socializing they do.

It was the psychologist C. Jung who coined the terms "extrovert" and "introvert" and who felt that the introvert often enjoys a rich inner life. Many creative people, including many actors, have this left-hand slope. Nancy Reagan's writing is a perfect example of the left-hand slope (page 17).

The three basic slopes of writing have been summed up as:

- right-slope = compliant
- upright = self-reliant
- left-slope = defiant

When looking at the slopes of your partner's and your own writing, do not despair if they are different. The difference indicates that the two of you will need to be very tolerant of each other's different degree of socializing. There is no one right answer in handwriting, or life and romance for that matter.

Nancy Reagan

Too promising for the 28E. Ronnie has some visiting Head of State I think. We'll get to that later the day!

I hope to see you soon –

Ronald

Nancy

Every letter of Nancy Reagan's writing is on the "F" slope. Even those people who know nothing of graphology might agree that, indeed, Mrs. Reagan has a somewhat cool, even aloof personality.

Use this information to better understand your relationships, not dictate them. Many a happy marriage is based on differences.

Exercise 1

Use the spaces on below to determine the slant of your own handwriting and to compare it to the slant of your loved one's writing. Each of you should write, in pencil: "I live in New York City and my name is…"

His

Hers

Chapter 2

Balance Between Ideals, Emotions, and Materialism

Claire and Tony

Claire had come to see me because she was concerned about her boyfriend Tony's career choices. She brought with her several samples of his writing that spanned the previous few months.

Looking at both his and her handwriting, I saw that in Claire's writing, all the letters were very much the same size. There were no big loops either above or below the letters. Her letters were quite wide and the ends of the words had little upward curves on them. These traits indicated to me that her priorities in life were friends, family, and home and also that she had a warm, emotional personality.

Tony's writing had none of these traits. His upper loops were excessively high and his under strokes came very far down in straight lines. The size of his small letters such as *a, o,* and *e* were tiny by comparison—all clearly indicating that his passion in life would always be his ideas and projects. The warmth and companionship of family and home were of no importance to him. The neglected small letters also indicated a frequent lack of attention to his personal well-being.

Claire was particularly interested in knowing whether Tony was likely to make a responsible, reliable, and caring husband. She was in her late 20s and had been working for the last five years as a personal assistant to the president of a clothing company. Although she enjoyed her work and liked being surrounded by beautiful clothes, her true desires were marriage and motherhood. She had been dating Tony for over a year at that point, with no sign of commitment, and she was concerned about their prospects. She felt that in his own way he cared for her deeply, but he constantly broke arrangements with her to finish one of his own projects.

His work record over the last few years was not reassuring because he had been employed by six different companies, none of which held any promising career prospects. He was very well educated, charming, intelligent, and full of ideas and plans, but he viewed his daytime job as an unpleasant necessity that allowed him to pursue his dream of being an inventor. Sadly, five years had passed with no sign of any of his projects being taken seriously.

Most days after work Tony went straight into his 'laboratory' in his father's garage and experimented with his latest idea. He rarely actually completed a project because he did tend to become bored easily by one project and then he would become too enthused by his next idea. Many times he would fall asleep while working and the next morning when he was running late for work, he would dash off without breakfast or a shower.

After analyzing Tony's handwriting and explaining all of his basic character traits to Claire, she came to accept that if she did want a caring, attentive husband, sadly, Tony would never be able to fulfill that role to her satisfaction. Not that he was an unkind man, but she would be a far second to his inventions, and that is not what she wanted.

A few months later, she returned with Darren's writing and I was happy to see that he was a much better match for her. I could immediately see in Darren's writing that it looked a lot like Claire's, with a distinct slope off to the right and an emphasis on the small letters.

The 2nd Secret for Finding Your Perfect Match:

Balance

The next thing we look for in handwriting is the part that will tell you if your loved one's interests are more idealistic (the intellectual and spiritual realms), emotional (biological and subconscious areas), or materialistic (ego). We find this by looking at the difference in size of the three different parts making up letters—also referred to as the "zones."

1. upper loops (that is, on the letters *d*, *t*, and so forth).
2. the lower loops (that is, on the letters *g*, *y*, and so forth).
3. the middle/small letters (that is, *o*, *a*, and so forth).

In a perfectly balanced example, these three "zones" are of equal height, but this is often not the case. There is, however, a very good example of balance between the three areas found in the writing of that old-time swashbuckling actor, Errol Flynn (page 23).

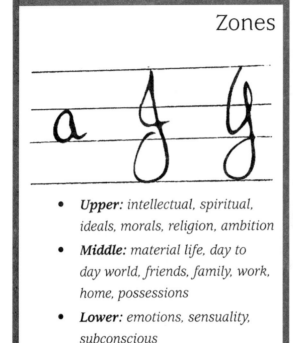

Zones

- **Upper:** *intellectual, spiritual, ideals, morals, religion, ambition*
- **Middle:** *material life, day to day world, friends, family, work, home, possessions*
- **Lower:** *emotions, sensuality, subconscious*

If you should notice that your loved one's writing has a noticeable emphasis on one area only, that does not mean that he is unbalanced, it just means that this part of his character has greater prominence.

Strong partnerships are frequently found when, for example, one person with a very high degree of imagination (high upper loops) teams up with a person who has the middle letters written much larger without much higher or lower loops. Such a person can provide a stabilizing force in the union.

When you notice that the upper loops are unusually high compared with the rest of the letters, you are dealing with a person whose attention is primarily on dreams, schemes, and projects. He is constantly striving towards his ideals and visions. This is the person with the overview of life—the "big picture" rather than someone dealing with the more everyday situations. The high upper loops may also indicate a person who is permanently day-dreaming. They may not complete any of their concepts because they tend to lack practical thought. (See Chapter 8 on ambition to ascertain possibility of success.)

Exaggerated upper loops are also to be found in very spiritual people who are "reaching for the heavens." Steve McQueen's letter (page 24) was written at a time when he was in Mexico seeking alternative health treatments. The sample "highly spiritual" belongs to a psychologist who has apparently been aware of her own past lives (in great detail) since she was a small child.

Errol Flynn

Miss Lowe /

Please call Mr. B... to say can't meet him tomorrow. Mrs. Flynn calls, please have George g... up instantly.

This handwriting sample is an almost perfect balance of the size of the upper, middle, and lower zones, indicating a balance in personality.

If you see very high upper loops with very small middle letters watch for the person who may get so carried away with their ideas that eating, sleeping, and changing their clothes may be forgotten. There is a danger of self-neglect, not to mention neglect of anyone else. Take care if your partner has this aspect, for

Highly Spiritual

I live in New York City and my name is

These very high upper and deep lower loops belong to someone aware of her past lives since childhood.

Steve McQueen

This sample was written in Mexico at a time when the actor was looking into alternative health cures, the very high upper slopes show inspiration and looking for things beyond the material.

relationships tend not to be of paramount importance. The sample "extreme lack of realism" (page 25) includes both unusually long upper and lower loops and was written by someone who had lost touch with reality.

The person whose letters are all much the same size as the small letters, with very few upper or lower loops, is someone who lives essentially in the moment as well as having an appreciation of the finer things in life. Many people trained in the arts write with the middle zone looking much larger than the rest of the letter. The writing of the brilliant Impressionist artist, Pissarro (page 27), is a perfect model of middle zone script. Emphasis on the middle zone will also often show us that this person is very practical and grounded in reality.

Very long lower loops show the depth of emotions and instincts and writers who can easily tap into their subconscious. Emphasis on the lower loops can indicate material desires and physical activity. There will also be evidence in these lower loops of emotional wholeness or barrenness. So the lower loops are very important in a personal relationship. They show attitudes to mother and father; painfully broken relationships; traumatic marriages, etc. (shown by very short, straight lines instead of loops). Not to mention, the person who, although they have experienced emotional problems, have made such great recovery that they are entirely able to fully enter

Extreme Lack of Realism

The very high and very low strokes hitting the lines both above and below tells of a person with little grasp of day to day reality.

into a new relationship (shown by a full sweep up at the end of the loop).

When the lower loops sweep off back to the left of the letter, this means that there is an extreme influence of mother and the early home life (not meant to be either a good or bad aspect, merely strong). A more moderate swing shows a person with traditional family values, again as learned from mother and perhaps maternal grandmother.

On the other hand, a lower loop curved back to the right shows a person whose father was physically or emotionally absent for the person as a child. This does not necessarily reflect the writer's level of affection towards the father. Jimi Hendrix's note (page 26) with its mixture of lower loops going both backwards and forwards is a clear indication of the trauma of his early life. The first five or so years he lived with his very isolated young mother and then alone with his father. An absent father in early life is

Jimi Hendrix

A very mixed style is presented here. On the one hand, the writing is wide showing a sociable person. However, the backward slopes of two of the ys indicated difficulties in childhood, the capital j and the y of "groovy" are too far to the left, indicating close ties to his mother. With such early problems showing, the ability to commit is in question.

shown in the backward sloping *y*'s. Early attachment to his mother is found in the extreme left slopes of the *J* in Jimi and the *g* in groovy.

A relationship in which one person has high-flying upper loops and long lower loops with the other partner having letters having large middle zones (with minimal upper and lower loops) requires patience from both people. The large "looped" person may feel restricted by the middle zone person who, in turn, may feel that her partner is all talk and ideas but of little use in the practical matters of life. As was said earlier though, these people do often gravitate towards each other to supply what they themselves may lack.

A final word on the lower sloops. It has traditionally been said that "sexiness" may be evaluated by the lower loops. This is a subject which could be a book all by itself but briefly put, I would ask you to think about what "sexiness" means? It is obviously as variable as people are themselves and it is my professional opinion that there are no truly reliable sexual indications to be found in handwriting. What is sexy to one person can be very off-putting to another!

Camille Pissarro

The Impressionist artist's letters are predominantly in the middle zone. This is the zone of all things material, and that always includes art and beauty. In this case, the letterform is not typical of his day.

Exercise 2

Write in script the following words: "Fighting equals less fun for everyone." Then look at the comparative sizes of the upper and lowers loops in such letters as the *f*, *g*, *h*, and *y*. Are these loops the same height as the letters *i*, *a*, and *e*?

His

Chapter 3

Connected to Others?

Pat, Richard, and the mother-in-law

P at and Richard had been happily married for 12 years. They both enjoyed successful careers and a busy social life. They had married a little later in life, so they did not have children, but found great joy in each other.

Everything had been going very well for them, up to the time when Richard's father had died and his mother was left alone. Richard had asked Pat what she thought about his mother coming to live with them because they certainly had enough room for her.

It was at this time that Pat came to see me and ask for my assistance. She got along well with her mother-in-law, but as is common in families, she had few opportunities to spend time alone with her. Pat was deeply worried that her marriage might suffer and she did not see herself being able to share Richard with his mother.

I looked at the writings from Pat, Richard, and his mother together to see if this potentially troubling

---

Letter Connections

- **Angular:** controlling, hard-headed, pugnacious.

- **Arcade:** diplomatic, inpenetratable.

- **Garland:** friendly, sociable, easy-going.

- **Thread:** avoids issues, can indicate deception.

(squiggles, impossible to duplicate)

---

situation could be made to work for all of them. Richard's script was in the style called *angular* (above), with very pointed letters indicating his rigid, rather opinionated attitude toward life. He was a highly respected historian and lectured at a large Ivy League college. The facility tended to feel more admiration than personal warmth toward him because the ability to compromise on any issue was alien to him.

By contrast, Pat's writing was in the very fluid style called *garland* (above). Many times garland style writing has been likened to a number of cups standing side by side. Friendly, sympathetic, and accommodating by nature, she owned a daycare center. In many ways, she dealt with Richard's prickly nature as if he were a temperamental 5-year-old, but did this in such a way that there was no disrespect of his abilities. She also tended to smooth over

Connected to Others

'Garland connections are wide at the bottom of the letters, and almost cup-like at the tops of such letters as 'n' and 'n'. This is the most sociable of the connections.

'Arcade' writing has wide arches on the top of such letters as 'm' and 'n' and indicates the diplomatic and cool character.

'ANGULAR' writing has pointed tops to the letters and shows a person with a very intellectual and sometimes hard-headed character.

Thread *connections are no more than an illegible squiggle across the paper (and impossible to duplicate in a readable fashion).*

the many people he had unknowingly offended. Although many found Richard to be too strict and controlling for their liking, Pat's relationship with him was possible in no small part because of her easygoing nature.

Richard's mother's script was in the *arcade* style (page 30); this type of letter connection looks as if a series of arches was drawn over the tops of letters. The arcade style has been likened to a number of cups turned upside down. People who use this style are considered to be the most diplomatic of people; somewhat formal in style, reserved, and not likely to interfere in other people's lives.

On seeing this interesting mixture of people, I felt sure that the basic structure of the marriage would not be damaged if they agreed to have the mother-in-law live with them. It was also particularly helpful that they lived in a house big enough to have a separate apartment which would suit Richard's mother perfectly, as she certainly did not want to be part of their everyday life. She was very active and had her own social circle and interests outside the home.

When Pat checked back with me a year later, she was very pleased by the way their arrangement was working out. Her mother-in-law was very independent and preferred to cook her own meals. Pat was finding, to her surprise, that she had to ask a few times before she could be persuaded to spend time with them.

The 3rd Secret for Finding Your Perfect Match:

Letter Connection

The next thing to look for in your partner's writing is the way in which the letters are connected to each other. This is yet another way to see how the writer deals with people and his or her immediate surroundings.

There are four basic types of connections between letters and they are, in order of most common use:

Garland connection, which is when the letters

Rae Dawn Chong

Rae Dawn Chong's writing is garland in style. Note the small n, and some m's, and the wide rounded bottoms of letters.

are joined to each other with wide and rounded bottoms and resemble a line of cups (or, a line of small *w*'s). These people are sympathetic to others, friendly, and generally easygoing in nature, lacking aggression. The tops of the small *n* and *m* are somewhat pointed at the top, but again, wide at the bottom. These writers tend to avoid conflict and can sometimes be easily led by stronger personalities. The actress Rae Dawn Chong's writing is a example of garland connections.

Arcade is the next most commonly used type of letter connection. Here the writing seems to have wide arches on the tops of the letters, particularly noticeable in the *m* and *n* (it also looks like garland connections, but upside down). The personality is reserved, secretive, and most diplomatic. These writers are difficult to get close to because they display a somewhat formal manner, which sometimes masks a shy personality used during social conventions to overcome a lack of ease with people. Where the arch is very wide, artistic, musical, or literary aptitude is very possible. Walter Lantz, the brilliant cartoonist, writes in the arcade style (page 34).

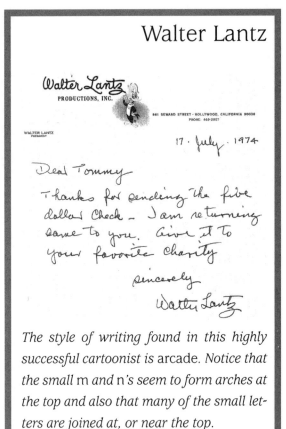

Walter Lantz

Walter Lantz
PRODUCTIONS, INC.

861 SEWARD STREET · HOLLYWOOD, CALIFORNIA 90038
PHONE: 469-2907

WALTER LANTZ
PRESIDENT

17 · July · 1974

Dear Tommy—

Thanks for sending the five dollar Check — I am returning same to you. Give it to your favorite Charity

Sincerely

Walter Lantz

The style of writing found in this highly successful cartoonist is arcade. *Notice that the small* m *and* n*'s seem to form arches at the top and also that many of the small letters are joined at, or near the top.*

You will notice that most of his small letters are joined at, or near the top of, the letter.

Angular is the third type of connection and is clearly seen in the very pointed and narrow nature of the letters. The man who writes in this style is also very much to the point in his manner and opinions—of which he has many! This person deals with facts, intellect, and realistic reasoning as opposed to emotions and intuition. These writers are very analytical, frequently rigid and disciplined, and often highly intelligent people. When the writing is extremely sharply pointed, the writer is very forceful in his point of view and is without too much regard for the sensitivities of others. He is also hard-working, uncompromising, and very tense by nature. These traits are coupled with great persistence and strength of will. Many literary people have this connection. Both the property developer Donald Trump and the Art Deco artist Erté share this style of writing (page 35).

Thread connection of writing is not frequently found (which is just as well, as it is almost impossible to read and writing is designed to be read after all). There seems to be little or no definition of any of the letters, merely a squiggle of a line, making it almost impossible to read. There is always something very secretive about these people and sometimes, but by no means always, there is something to hide. Avoidance of responsibility is also a possibility. On the other hand, thread writing is found in very fast-thinking people and also in many very intelligent, versatile people whose work demands that they write a lot and very quickly—doctors, for example.

Donald Trump

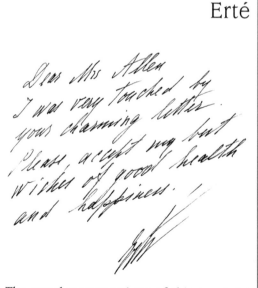

A perfect example of angular connections with sharp points on the top of the letters. It is clear that this is a person who demands everything on his own terms.

Erté

The angular connections of this great Art Deco artist reflect the lines often found in his work.

Other times the thread connection is found in those writers with a problem in decision-making. The more breaks there are in thread writing, the more reliable the character. Breaks refer to the gaps between some of the words, where there is no continual line of writing, with each word joined to the next.

Exercise 3

Both of you need to write, in script, the following sentence: "Mutual money marketing makes profits." Check the shape of the *m* and *n* in particular to see which letter connection you both have.

His

_____

Hers

_____

Chapter 4

Sociable or Aloof?

Emily and Clive

Emily's anxious personality was clearly evident at our first meeting. She was very overwrought, having had a disagreement with her cab driver, and she could not stop talking. When we had been on the phone earlier to arrange our appointment, she had been reluctant to conclude the conversation.

When I first looked at her writing, it was very hard to make out the words, as they almost ran into each other. Not only that, but the upper and lower loops collided with the lines of writing above and below. These are the classic signs of someone whose desperate need for companionship is the very thing that drives people away. This causes a vicious circle because rejection makes her try even harder to impress and please. The need for someone, almost anyone, to be with her, clouded her ability to choose friends wisely.

She was an attractive woman in her mid-30s, but her anxious need to connect with people was all too apparent even at the briefest meeting. Interestingly, she came from a large family, but had been neglected by her parents, particularly her father.

She came to see me because she had met Clive, a writer, at a social event in a local museum and although they had attended a few lectures together, she felt no sense of warmth from him. She was already deeply concerned that she had done something to displease him and wanted to know if she could correct the situation because she liked him a lot.

Emily had, by mistake, picked up a page of notes Clive had taken at one of the lectures they had been to and this was what she gave me to analyze. His writing showed a very different use of space on the page than hers. Each word was very far away from the next, also each line was very separate from the lines above and below. Each of his letters were very narrow with very straight backs to them. Without a doubt, Clive was a deeply reserved, private person who was perfectly happy with his own company.

In advising Emily, I had to very carefully suggest to her that her constant efforts to please people, followed by unreasonable demands on their time, was not very helpful to her and had not brought her much happiness. People felt bombarded by her calls, gifts, and eventual demands. As tactful as I tried to be, I knew she felt insulted because she truly believed that her behavior was a sign of caring. Over the next year, however, she did enter therapy to work on these issues.

About 18 months later, when she returned to see me, I was interested to note that her writing was beginning to show signs of moderation. She had realized that her friendship with Clive was a casual one. She had widened her social activities to include more group situations, which she found to be less stressful. Over a period of time, she felt ready to try a more intimate relationship and did find someone she is happy with.

Spacing

I live in New York City and my name is

I live in New York city. My name is

I live in New York City & My name is:

The first sample is of normal spacing, the second is of wide spacing, and the third sample is somewhat crowded.

The 4th Secret for Finding Your Perfect Match:

Spacing

When we look at the amount of space between words, we are also looking at the amount of space a person prefers around them. An equal, moderate amount of space indicates a well-balanced personality. The "spacing" sample on the top of the page shows what would be considered normal, wide, or crowded spacing. Ideally, the amount of space between words should be the width of one letter.

Extremely elongated spacing between both individual words and lines reveals a person who is trying very hard

Queen Alexandra

This is a clear example of unnecessary lines linking one word to the next. This is an attempt to keep people at bay. This is, of course, a regal attribute.

to remove himself from the company of others. These writers view other people with a certain amount of initial mistrust, as if fearing invasion of his personal space. He may find it difficult to connect emotionally with too many people, which does not imply that such people are incapable of love, merely very choosy. Many highly creative people have this trait of isolation because they need peace and tranquillity to concentrate on their talent. If this is a new trend in a person, it should be viewed with some caution, as it might be an unhealthy sign of isolation due to emotional pressures.

If in writing with overly long spacing there are also lines connecting one word to the next, this person has put up barbed wire to keep people away. Queen Alexandra's inscription of a book to her grandson (above) has these unnecessary lines between words. In a member of a royal family this distance is to be expected, but it is not so desirable in a love partner unless you yourself crave an equal amount of space.

Another characteristic of the person with the very wide spacing between words is that they have an actual need to live in large spaces. It is not just a preference, but an absolute requirement. Looking at each word and seeing it so detached and isolated from its neighboring words gives great insight into the writer. Gloria Vanderbilt's sample (right) clearly shows how an artist requires peace and tranquillity to create. In a similar way, the actor Terence Stamp's note (right) shows a mixture of both very wide and normal spacing, indicating a varied need for people and solitude.

Gloria Vanderbilt

Here the wide spacing between the words indicates the peace and tranquility needed by a highly creative artist.

Terence Stamp

This very intense actor's writing has a mixture of very wide and normal spacing indicating a varying degree of sociability.

Aloof

I leave in New-York-city and hame is

I live in New york.

My name is

The very wide spacing of these two samples show us people who prefer fresh air around them rather than people.

The "aloof" sample (above) is of two people with unusually large spaces between their words and lines. The "interesting mixture" sample (page 45) displays an unusual blend of wide spacing between the words and a rather flamboyant letter style indicating, yet again, an artistic temperament with a need for solitude in order to create.

Writing that looks very crowded is found in needy people, usually wanting company at all times and is playing a lack of discrimination, self-sufficiency, and independence. If the words are packed in tightly one beside the next and if the upper and lower loops run into the lines above and below, rest assured that this person will frequently have no regard for other people's space and privacy. Their harried writing reflects their treatment of people—they will run them over at times of high anxiety. During these times there is no regard for the convenience of someone else because the overwhelming needs of the neurotic person takes priority in their minds. For example, they may call a friend at 3 a.m. with no thought that she has to get up at 7 a.m. to go to work. Their justification, if they think of it at all, is that they would be available in the same way.

Interesting Mixture

There are signs of flamboyance in the letters, yet the words are widely spaced.

The "overcrowding" sample (below) is of a person functioning well enough professionally, but who is overly needy for personal companionship, often to his detriment. To crave attention from almost anyone is not a healthy trait. The sample "total lack of discrimination" (page 46) on the other hand, was written by someone not functioning well at all. The writer was desperately trying to form a link with me after

Overcrowding

The problem here could well be the desire to have anyone at all around, rather than being by oneself. There is almost a fear of being alone even for a short period of time.

Total Lack of Discrimination

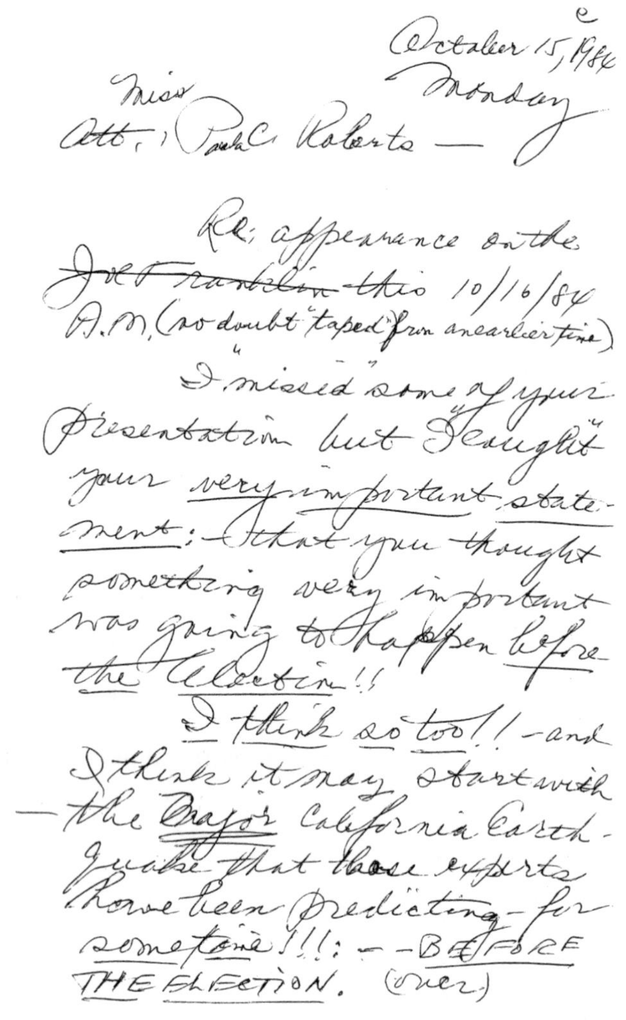

[handwritten letter]

October 15, 1984
Monday

Miss,
Att'n, Paul C. Roberts —

Re: appearance on the
~~Joe Franklin~~ this 10/16/84
A.M. (no doubt "taped" from an earlier time)
I "missed" some of your
presentation but I caught"
your *very important* statement: that you thought
something *very important*
was going to happen before
the election!!

I think so too!! — and
I think it may start with
— the major California Earth-
quake that those experts
have been predicting — for
sometime!!! — BEFORE
THE ELECTION. (over)

This sample is very crowded and is from someone trying desperately hard to make a connection to someone. In fact, to anyone really. The need to be with other people is more acute than what could be considered normal.

having seen me briefly on a television show. To be so needy for personal contact that they would try to forge a link with a stranger on a television screen is not normal. The totally cramped letters are falling over themselves and each other in a way that is no longer neighborly.

In looking for a healthy relationship, look for a partner whose writing displays the letters and lines that are neither too wide nor too close together. Either extreme indicates an unusual attitude to socializing. The one exception to this rule might be when your own writing has very wide spacing, in which case you are likely to appreciate another somewhat isolated person. The choice, as always, is yours.

Exercise 4

You and your loved one need to write, in script: "All sociable people stick together."

Check to see if the words are placed either too closely (less than letter-width) together, or unusually far apart.

His

Hers

Chapter 5

Flamboyant or Modest?

Bob and Juliette

Bob had been a client of mine for many years. He had weathered an early disappointing marriage and was now in his late 30s. He had worked hard in his father's accounting firm and had become a full partner. Upon first impression, he certainly would not appear to be as successful as he is. His manner is quiet and his clothing is very conservative.

Bob's writing is as careful and modest as he is himself. Each letter is small and precisely formed with every i-dot neatly in place and each t-bar attached to the upright stroke of the letter. The sample of his friend's, which he had brought me, was truly a work of art with all of it's curves, curls, and flourishes, not to mention it's enormous size. The two styles of writing, and therefore, characters, could not have been more different.

Bob wanted to talk to me about this new lady in his life, Juliette. A month prior to our meeting, he had quite by chance bumped into a client,

John, after work who persuaded him to go and have a drink. They went to a very fashionable bar full of attractive people. Bob's client immediately started to talk to two young women at the bar. Bob was very shy and almost embarrassed by this. Nevertheless, one of the two women seemed to take a liking to him and insisted on calling him Roberto. He did not know why she had taken to calling him that, but he did not have the opportunity to find out because he had to leave for an evening meeting. He did, however, manage to give her his card.

To his great surprise, Juliette called him the next day and asked him to accompany her to an opening night at the local theatre. Out of politeness, he accepted. Once he was there, Bob was in awe of Juliette's boldness in approaching people during the intermission. She introduced him to everyone she spoke to. He found out that evening that she was an actress who was quite well known. He was feeling very flattered and almost honored to be in the company of such a glamorous person.

Since that first evening, they had been to several events at each of which Juliette was the center of attention. Bob was really beginning to enjoy this very different lifestyle but wondered if she would find him boring in time. I explained to him that in an unusual way, he and Juliette may be perfect together. In her profession and with her exuberant personality, she would have found it easy to find a friend in her own field, but she had chosen him. Why? Perhaps, very simply, because she had enough bounce and vigor for two and was looking for safety and security in a man who also did not try to compete with her socially.

He was enthralled by her and she in turn adored his attention and steadfastness. The last I heard was that they are happily married and continuing to enjoy their contrasting natures.

The 5th Secret for Finding Your Perfect Match:

Size and Embellishment

The modest or flamboyant character is shown simply in the size of the writing and sometimes in the embellishment of it. (A lot of the rules of handwriting analysis are surprisingly simple and particularly so here.) Big, bold letters indicate a big, bold nature. Well, if not always bold, certainly on the louder side. Dramatic people use flourishes in their manner, dress, voice, and writing. The sample "showy" (below) is from a restauranteur whose establishments were always very dramatic. The extraordinary escape artist, Houdini (page 52), had writing that displays a mixture of control, independence, and showmanship—exactly as he was!

A more modest, unassuming person will also quite simply have small, understated writing. Almost not wanting to disturb anyone else, the letters are undersized and humble. On no account does

Showy

The larger than life writing of a well-known restaurateur.

this mean under-achievement, though. British Beatle John Lennon's writing (right) is quite small and precise, but his artistic achievements are unquestionable.

Great intellectual and scholastic achievement is often accompanied by very small writing—meaning a highly concentrated mind and a person with no interest in impressing the general public with their worth. The sample "unassuming" (page 53) illustrates this point. Also, President Ronald Reagan's sample (page 53) shows nothing of what one might expect from a leader of the free world. Many people might imagine that a head of state would have large and entrepreneurial writing, but this is often not the case. Upon

John Lennon

> Belle: Al Green.
> I can't stand the Rain
> Ann Peebles.
> Do ya think I'm sexy: R. Stewart!
> Miss You: MR JAGGER.
> You make me Feel Mighty Real
> (Sylvester?)

This small, left-sloping and disconnected writing belongs to this complex musician and writer. A thoughtful and reclusive person in his life away from performing.

Houdini

> Love Laughs at Lockensmiths
> So does
> Harry Houdini

The upward sweep at the end of "laughs" is typical of the person who can perform in front of groups of people.

Unassuming

Readers handle their own money; fees, charge what they want, at least $15 for a mini-reading, 15 minutes or so. Some readers charge $20, $25 or more. That's up to you. You make your own time schedule and change what you wish. (Bring yourself some change) at the end of the day split 50%-50% with us. Believe me, you will do very well!

The small, neat writing shown here seems to belong more to an academic person than to someone trying to organize a psychic fair.

reflection, might it be wise to have a cool, collected, thoughtful person to wield such power?

If you notice that your loved one's writing is small and simple in style, this will mean that he is also somewhat reserved in manner. This by no means indicates that he does not like to enjoy himself, but do not look for him to be center-stage too often. Accountants' writing is often undersized, with each letter being very carefully formed and legible. All the *i*'s are dotted and the *t*'s neatly crossed. In their highly detailed and exacting work, such precision is essential. Remember that many highly successful heads of corporations had a basic training in finance. An

Ronald Regan

Again thanks & best of luck

Sincerely

Ronald Reagan

This writing is small and remarkably modest. Not what one might have expected from the leader of the free world.

Jayne Mansfield

Everything in this sample is as lively as the personality of its writer. Even the little heart shows a warmth of character and a very theatrical flair.

understanding of money can lead to great wealth without any grandiose behavior.

When your partner's writing is noticeably larger than normal and perhaps also has a certain amount of unnecessary flourishes, you have found yourself with a person who likes to be noticed at all times. The writing itself cannot tell you whether or not the writer is worthy of notice, but only that he loves the limelight. Both of the actresses, Jayne

Arlene Dahl

This larger than life writing, which has the "orator's swing" at the end of some words, perferctly reflects this actress's sense of style and theatrics.

Mansfield (page 54) and Arlene Dahl (above) show strong theatrical flair.

Although they are so fundamentally different, can a modest person get on well with a more flamboyant character? This is one basic difference between people where the two can complement each other well. After all, what is the joy in being ostentatious and vibrant if there is no audience to play to? Many a reticent person may secretly admire the boldness of his friend while in no way wishing to be like him. The more

Georgia O'Keefe

This oversized handwriting is full of flourishes and is every bit as vibrant as colorful as the artist's work.

Mick Jagger

Dear Helen,

Thanks a lot for your letter, also for the *[jumper?]*. Yes I do like it.

Hope you like "Paint it Black".

We're doing a tour of Britain in September then I that we're coming to Ireland. Must go now,

Love,

Mick Jagger

The left slope of the writing, together with the disconnected letters tells us of a character a lot more analytical, intuitive, and away from the world than his stage manner would suggest. The exuberance illustrated by the very large capital letters is what is seen by the public.

theatrical person may find much to rely on in the steady, quiet, modest person.

It must not be automatically presumed that the larger the writing, the more accomplished a person is. Certainly big writing can

Flamboyant or Modest?

I demand to be noticed

Oversized writing, sometimes coupled with unnecessary flour-ishes, is found in people very anxious to be seen and heard. In itself, this writing does not indicate whether the writer has any special achievements worthy of notice.

I am quiet, modest and self

assured of my achievements

without any particular interest

in anyone else noticing me or not.

Undersized writing is often found in very successful people, as well as quiet, unassuming people. Sometimes these writers have done very well in school but have no interest in broadcasting this.

be found in people whose achievements are also noticeable but that tends to depend upon what career they have chosen. In the case of Georgia O'Keefe (page 55), the flamboyant style is cer-tainly reminiscent of her bold artwork. In another case, the sample "flamboyant" (page 58) the writer's desire to be special in the public eye is not matched with abilities to achieve this recogni-tion. Interestingly enough, Mick Jagger's onstage persona is only reflected in the large capital letters in his writing (page 56). This indicates a desire to be noticed, but only when it suits him.

Another mark of a partner's self-esteem is found in the way he writes a capital *I*, referring to himself. If you can see that this letter is much the same as his other capital letters, it marks a reasonable ego. If, on the other hand, it is considerably larger, then you are dealing with an inflated sense of self and you need to consider

Flamboyant

I live in New York City. & my name is

The overly embellished flourishes in this example indicates a very strong desire to impress other people. This client does not have the ability to achieve the inflated idea of self and is living in a fantasy world. Notice how the upper and lower loops run into the lines both above and below; this indicates a lack of boundaries.

whether this is a trait you would be able to accept in a life partner. Also, when you see this very large personal *I* with other signs of a flamboyant character, this writer tends not to be very sensitive to the feelings of others—including you.

In very rare cases, the personal *I* is written as a small letter and this shows a degree of an inferiority complex. These people need a great deal of encouragement in life, but if you are a very supportive person, this will unlikely be an obstacle to you.

Exercise 5

To check whether the sizes of both of your handwritings vary greatly, write out in script: "Larger than life people have dramatic writing."

His

Hers

Chapter 6

Moody or Stable?

Sarah and her boss

When Sarah came for her appointment, she told me that she wanted to check the level of compatibility with a work colleague. I do not ask clients anything about themselves before working on their handwriting sample or any other person's they have brought with them. Sometimes, however, people do want to point out whether the issue is personal or professional.

Sarah told me that she had recently completed a degree in nursing and was going to enter the field of pediatrics, as she loved children. She had been delighted to find an entry-level position in a nearby hospital. Her reason for seeking my advice was that she needed to know if there was a way in which she could better relate to the senior nurse in her department. This woman's behavior was making her miserable; one day she would be bright and cheerful, the next, for no apparent reason, full of gloom and criticism.

Sarah did not know how to deal with these unpredictable mood swings and was beginning to feel that perhaps she was causing the problem in some way. As she obviously had a wonderful temperament, this was unlikely. She had only been working at the hospital for a few months and already her confidence in her skills was slipping. She was losing sleep worrying about the problem with her boss and did not want to think that her job performance might suffer.

Looking first at Sarah's handwriting, I saw that it was very evenly sized and that all the lines went straight across the page (neither sloping up nor down). All these were strong signs of an even, stable temperament. The several samples she showed me of her supervisor told a very different story. Even in the same line of writing, the letters were formed in many different ways. Also, some of the samples had lines in which the writing took a markedly upward swing. Other samples written on different days had the writing drooping way down at the end of the lines. Her boss was certainly displaying very erratic mood swings.

Because Sarah did not want to transfer to another department or hospital and her supervisor seemed to be a permanent fixture, we had to work out a way in which she would feel more comfortable at work. The first thing I made very clear to her was that she must not think that the mood swings were in any way caused by her, as they were not. She did not contribute to her boss's moods, nor could she prevent them. Until she fully understood that, she would continue to unnecessarily blame herself.

We then discussed how she could diplomatically tell her boss that her bad moods were undermining the work performance in her own department. Sarah did find the courage to set up a meeting, choosing one of the senior nurse's better days, and told her how much she was affected by the constantly changing reaction to her work. She politely asked if there was anything she could do about it.

The supervisor was somewhat taken by surprise, although she was enough of a professional to realize that she was causing the problem. She was aware of her moodiness but somehow believed that everyone understood that it was "just her way" and took no notice of it. She did not go as far as to apologize to Sarah, but she did assure her that she was a very valuable member of the team and she certainly did not want to lose her.

The 6th Secret for Finding Your Perfect Match:

Direction Across Page

A very important thing to look for in a relationship is the varying moods of the other person and your own level of tolerance of any such swings. One can go back to the old Chinese adage: "bored to death or worried to death." The stability and constancy of a person's moods affects everyone around them.

When someone is calm and steady most of the time, we find we can rely on them. We know that her moderation of temperament shows a reliability that we can count on. That state may be optimistic, pessimistic, or somewhere in between, but we will know what to expect from that person. This calm personality does not mean that someone is flat, dull, or without emotional reactions, but that there is a basic composure and grounding. The sample "stability of mood" (page 64) clearly shows that the line of writing goes in a straight line across the page. These people may, or may not be, pleasant, but whatever their usual way of being, there is little variation from that state of mind.

If, however, you are dealing with someone who constantly exhibits a different mood, this is very difficult to deal with. If you are of a somewhat temperamental nature yourself, it will be easier for you to understand another person's similar ups

Stability of Mood

I live in New York City and my name is

Diane Baker

The writing of this successful actress goes in a perfectly straight line across the page, indicating a very even temperament.

and downs. This does not automatically mean that you will like these mood changes or that they are the same as your own. However, if you are of a calmer, more reasonable nature, dealing with what you would think of as temper tantrum could be very wearing. Equally, the bright, breezy, eternally sunny person might find the more pessimistic person a constant drain on their energies.

The more erratic character is on a constant roller coaster, making it hard for others to gauge their present mood. Certainly from one day to the next there are great swings and these do not seem to correspond to any particular event. One day a moody person will appear cheerful, upbeat, and optimistic. The next day, they are grouchy, despondent, and sullen again for no apparent reason. When we put together the more consistent person with the more volatile partner, there are great misunderstandings. It would be hard for the more moderate person to accept that the loved one's moods are not a result of anything that has happened between the two of them.

On average, we all have a more or less set degree of optimism or pessimism. What that means is that if a basically optimistic

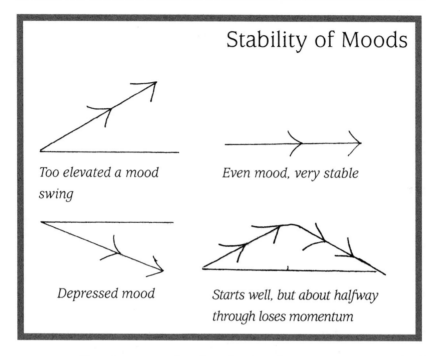

Stability of Moods

Too elevated a mood swing

Even mood, very stable

Depressed mood

Starts well, but about halfway through loses momentum

person suffered an emotional setback, after a certain period of time, he or she would return to their normal emotional state of being. In the same way, if a basically pessimistic person had a period of great happiness, they would still revert to their less joyful personality. In any relationship, only those two people concerned can really say if they feel better with someone else of like moods, or if they prefer the contrast provided by someone with an opposite temperament. This is only for you to decide.

To find this aspect, the handwriting sample must be on unlined paper. The reason for this is, we must draw a horizontal line under the writing to see if it is on an invisible straight course across the page. If it is, then he has an even temperament and is a person who literally follows a straight path in life. Any variation from this indicates mood swings. When the line under the writing swings up to the right, this shows an elated mood of the moment. This mood will come down later! Both Joe Namath's

Three Very Different States of Mind

you need to put spe sheets into A-2 for 5 employees at Buff Color (or Black body).

Please don't even murmur That I am short of money because my business depends on people who think I'm well off! Only you know. Many thanks.

I live in New York City and My name is

The first sample is "flying high" way up to the right indicating a very upbeat mood at the time. The second sample droops right down at the end of the lines and the letter does talk of severe money problems. The third sample starting up and then trailing off tells of a person who starts projects with sufficient enthusiasm then has trouble finishing them.

Criminal

I need to get a lawyer in New York to take on my case. But I am hampered at getting in touch with such a lawyer due to my location and situation.

There fore, I decided to write upon you in all hope and sincerity that you can and will assist me in obtaining a New York Bar Attorney Directory. It sure should be deeply appreciated.

I sincerely hope this letter finds you in good health and much happiness.

Thank you for your help in this matter. Please answer at your earliest convenience.

This letter, written by a prison inmate, is too precise and orderly. A ruler could be put on the back of all these letters and they would be found to be the same. In this case, it clearly indicates an obsessional personality needing professional guidance.

(page 69) and Dan Quayle's (page 70) letters swing up to the right, but not so dramatically to suggest anything more than natural exuberance. These moods of the moment will also return to the straight line across the page indicating a stable personality.

If the line under the writing droops down toward the corner of the page, you are looking at a depressed state. Hemingway's note was written just four months before he took his own life and it is on a decidedly downward slope (page 70). Ideally, to judge moods, we need to see several samples written over a period of time. We must remember that a person might be going through a particularly hard time so that a depression is understandable and temporary. When this droop downward is seen for some

---

Very Erratic Letterform

London, 17/10-74

10.30

We have just been here, we are going to try to find your telephone number (because I have forgotten it in the flat) and try to telephone you in the Gallery. We will be back in about an hour.

Even on such a short note, there are corrections for words left out. As this was not written by a child, when you see such low letterforms and omissions, there is reason to be wary.

---

time, it is usually wise to consider urging the person toward professional help rather than believing that our own loving care will improve their state.

There are times when a person may be very stable and later in life slip into despair. Mark Rothko's sample shows a steady flow across the page with no sign at this time of the descent, which led him to suicide (page 72).

When the line starts to go up and then descends sharply, there is a problem with following through on projects, even those started with great enthusiasm. There is constant uncertainty with these people and often a great sense of insecurity. A sample of this first going up and then down with the same line is shown in the sample "three states of mind" (page 66).

Although the intentions of this book are to draw attention to the positive parts of a person's nature, there are a few warning

Joe Namath

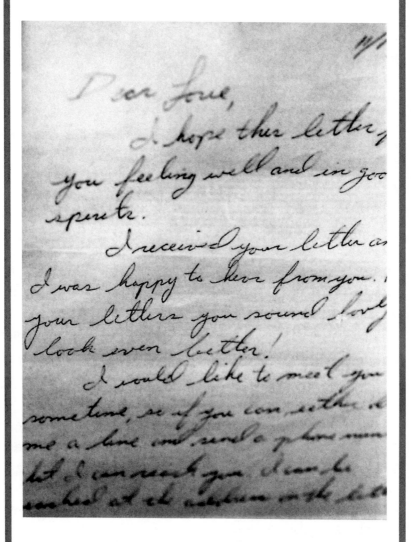

In this letter, written in his bachelor days, this dynamic football player displays a liking for people with his writing's strong swing to the right. The lines slop up a little, showing a positive mood.

signs to be aware of. Apart from the lines under a writing either going in an exaggerated line up or down, when there is extremely unusual letter forms or letter slopes which are noticeably too uniform, caution is advised. The sample "criminal" (page 67) is a classic case of abnormally even backs of the letters—you could take a ruler to them and find that they are all in a perfectly straight line. The writer has an extremely obsessive nature.

Dan Quayle

Dear

I won't listen to 'em! I like fighting back. There's no shoo-in thingy here - never has been All Best — Guy

Here the upswing of the lines (and mood) are reflected in the words. He truly was in a positive state of mind.

Finally, the samples found in "very erratic letter form" (page 68) and "severe health and emotional problems" (page 71) were all written by people with such conflicts and psychological problems, that none of them could be thought of as potential partners

Ernest Hemmingway

To Hugh Best with sincere good wishes

Ernest Hemingway

The downward slope of the writing indicates the depressed mood. This was written just four months before he took his life.

Severe Health and Emotional Problems

I Live New York City

and my Name is

Hire I live in New York City my name is

I live in New York city and my name

Each of these writings belong to people with extremely serious problems. In these cases we have to say, sadly, that no one is compatible with them as they are very conflicted within themselves.

Mark Rothko

Am sorry to disappoint you about the Rosicrucian Society. But I do wish that it would seem pointless to me to devote oneself to the practice of an art whose nature is not "cosmic", if I understand the word correctly

Sincerely Mark Rothko.

P.S. I would appreciate the earliest possible return of the photographs which you find you cannot use.

At the time this was written, there was nothing to indicate the later depression which caused this artist to take his life. Here the writing is firm, with a forward movement and the lines go straight across the page. Writing does change, as the personality changes.

of any sort at that time. Strictly speaking, they are not compatible with themselves, let alone anyone else.

Exercise 6

For this exercise, both of you need to write out: "I wonder if my moods go up and down."

Take a ruler and place it underneath the line of writing to see if the writing goes straight across the page or slopes either up or down.

_____

Hers

_____

Chapter 7

Open or Secretive?

Lorenzo and Mary

L orenzo came to see me on the advice of a friend of his, whom I had helped with sorting out prospective employees through their handwritten applications. He was still quite young, only two years out of college, and had questions about his childhood sweetheart, Mary. They had been friends for years and always believed that they would marry someday. Although he did not doubt that, he found her behavior mysterious at times.

His handwriting has an almost childlike quality to it. All the letters are very rounded and legible, with all of the small *o*'s and *a*'s open at the tops. He is a person who is very receptive to people and ideas. He lets most things flood in and then he sifts through all the information before making his decisions. Another way of looking at this is that he is gullible by nature, wishing to always believe the best of everyone.

Mary's writing, by contrast, has all the small *o*'s and *a*'s very tightly closed off with little circles at the tops. She is not easily influenced by others and is deeply secretive by nature, the sort of girl who would not give her best friend the name of her hairdresser. Another interesting facet of her character is her ability to quickly and accurately sum up people at the first meeting. All this is shown, very simply, by the writing of the small *o*'s and *a*'s.

When Lorenzo was away at college, he called Mary quite often, but did not always find her at home. He was not at all a controlling type of personality, but if he ever asked her where she had been, she was very evasive. Indeed, sometimes she became quite angry and accused him of not trusting her. This problem with communication had continued and things had begun to get out of hand.

He felt that in asking her what she had been doing, he was expressing an interest in her well-being. As he rarely got an answer, he was beginning to wonder if he had made a mistake and could indeed trust her to be true to him.

When two people such as this form a bond, they must both learn to respect the one's need for privacy and the other's need for information. Neither will truly understand the motivations of the other, but it is essential to know that being secretive is not the same as being deceptive. That Mary does not choose to tell Lorenzo that she enjoys spending Thursday evenings shopping for her elderly aunt, does not mean that she would ever use it as an excuse to see someone else.

Lorenzo would need time to accept this, if he chooses to, and not to automatically think that there is something odd going on. Mary would need to accept that his enquiries are his way of showing interest, affection, and concern for her.

Recently he told me that they had decided to wait another year before discussing wedding plans.

The 7th Secret for Finding Your Perfect Match:

Letter Openings

It is very easy to determine if a person is open and trusting (and probably naïve), or is far more guarded in their dealings with people. Traditionally, this was also the part in handwriting analysis used to gauge a person's honesty, but I have found that not to be reliable. After all, a person may be scrupulously honest in dealing with money, while at the same time they are deceptive in love situations. Also, a very disturbed childhood may cause a person to be extremely cautious and secretive, but that does not mean that they are dishonest.

Having said that, let's look at tops of the small letters *o* and *a*. When they have an opening at the top of the letter, the person also is very open to ideas, people, and concepts in a trusting and often almost intuitive manner. The trusting, artless person is not to be thought of as totally naïve. His ability to be open and responsive to people and suggestions does not imply that he will totally believe everything that he is told. Nor is he indiscreet at all times.

When the tops of these *o* and *a*'s are covered with a little circle, that person is very discreet, secretive, and cautious. By the way, they are usually very accurate with their first impressions of people. The sample "extreme discretion" (page 79) is a very good illustration of this trait, as is the sample "journalist" (page 79). When you discover that you are with someone who is very private and seems to keep a lot from you, it is essential for your own

Open or Secretive?

The open top of letters, particularly the small a and o's, is found in the writing of people who let in other people, ideas, and suggestions. They are often somewhat gullible.

The closed "enrolled" tops of such small letters as a and o, show us a person who is discrete, guarded, and usually secretive in his manner. He is not often taken advantage of by others.

When you see the letter k with an unnecessary "covering" stroke down its back, this is the writing of a person guarding themselves a little too carefully.

well-being that you do not always presume something illicit is going on. Such people will always be reluctant to reveal much about themselves, even to those they love dearly. It may take you years to find out that those mysterious missing hours on Saturday mornings were, in fact, spent tutoring a literacy class. You may still be furious because you feel that you should have been told. Maybe so, but you must accept that you were not and will not be. The suppression of even trivial information is a basic part of this secretive personality and this will always be a mystery to the more open person.

Extreme Discretion

Note all the tightly closed tops of the a's and o's, showing all the prudence needed by an attorney.

When you see a writing has the little *a*'s and *o*'s with open tops showing a possible gullible person, this will not mean that he has nothing he might wish to conceal from you. He will generally be quite willing to

Journalist

The tightly closed a's show a person whose initial reactions to people are very accurate, which is vital to his work.

discuss his life and opinions with you.

Alternatively, if your loved one's writing shows tightly knotted tops of the little *a*'s and *o*'s, this does not mean he is holding many secrets from you, but he is certainly discreet and cautious about revealing too much too soon. Great care must be taken in judging another person's nature too quickly and coming to the wrong conclusion that they are

Sally Jessy Raphael

The open tops of most of this talk show host's o's and a's tells us that she is indeed open and sympathetic to her guests.

not straightforward in their dealings. It may well be that someone may take some period of time before they feel comfortable enough to share certain information with you.

The talk show host, Sally Jessy Raphael (above), is an example of an air of openness that allows her guests to feel comfortable in expressing their feelings to her. She is a perfect example of a person who is both trusting by nature and also a very successful businessperson. Being trusting of others certainly does not mean that a person lacks good judgment. This open quality is often found in people whose great charm and empathy has

Tom Brokaw

NBC

Many thanks for your generous comments in Forbes — January 11. It was a memorable week — & I'm pleased you watched. Best for '88

Tom

This respected newsman's writing has a mixture of partly open and partly closed small a's and o's. This means that he has a healthy balance between being open to possibilities and people while at the same time not being naive.

brought them great achievement. News-man Tom Brokaw (page 81) has a mixture of both openness and confidentiality in his writing, literally showing that at times he is more trusting than at other times.

Cindy Adams, know as the "Queen of Gossip" has in fact tightly encircled tops on her small o's and a's, telling us that she is the very soul of discretion when entrusted with private information (right). This is the same aspect that indicates that her initial impressions of people are very reliable. The financial genius, Malcolm Forbes, shared this sign of great discretion, allowing people to confide highly confidential material to him (page 83).

In your quest for the ideal partner, as much time should be spent looking at yourself as at the other person. You may

Cindy Adams

Cindy Adams is known as the "Queen of Gossip" but the tightly enclosed tops of a and o shows that she has all the discretion needed for people to trust her implicitly.

Malcom Forbes

FORBES MAGAZINE

CHAIRMAN & CHIEF EXECUTIVE OFFICER
EDITOR-IN-CHIEF

Friday Sept 16

Dearest

Happy Birthday to a wonderful, wondrously great lady!

Much much love,

Malcolm

FORBES BUILDING　　60 FIFTH AVENUE　　NEW YORK, N.Y. 10011　　212/620-2285

This financial wizard's writing has very carefully closed tops of the a's *and* o's, *indicating his very secretive nature.*

recognize that you are a rather guarded, cagey person yourself, who is enchanted by a trusting and gullible mate. This combination could bring out the protective and nurturing side of your nature, or it could spell disaster!

Exercise 7

For this exercise you need to write: "Am I open and accepting of others, or more closed and secretive?"

Look carefully at the tops of the small *a* and *o*'s to see if they are open or closed at the tops.

_____

Hers

_____

Chapter 8

Leader or Follower?

Rachel and Mark

New in town, Rachel had taken a temporary job in a computer firm to give her time to acclimate to her new surroundings. She had moved into an apartment with four other young women, to see where she might like to live before committing to a lease of her own.

Rachel gave me a sample of her own handwriting together with a sample of someone she was wondering if she was compatible with. Her writing sloped to the right with prominent small letters, indicating that she was the perfect team/support person. The other sample was typical of the highly driven businessman, with very high upper loops and high flying t-bars—all signs of an entrepreneurial personality.

Apparently, after a few weeks at her new job, she had confided in a roommate that she had taken a liking to her newly divorced boss, but felt sure that he had not noticed her at all. This was when she heard of me and decided to have his writing analyzed to see if a match was at all likely. Their situation was purely professional, but they shared a sense of humor and had found that they came from the same state and much the same sort of family background.

In discussing the differences with Rachel, I explained to her that more often than not, highly driven business people find loving partners in more quiet, behind-the-scenes kind of people. They generally do not look for competition on the home front. Which is not to say that two extremely ambitious people never get together, but they often have huge clashes of temperament because both egos need to be center stage.

When matching up the ambitious person with the more supportive partner, there is a very important aspect that Rachel would have to recognize. That is, should this interest develop into a relationship, she would, more often than not, be the one making the compromises. That is not to say that she would be a doormat, but the dynamics of this pairing are such that it would not work out well if she frequently challenged Mark's authority. Team-support people, such as Rachel, are the most likely to strive for compromise rather than conflict, so this would not be a problem.

As Mark's work would always remain a focal point in his life, she would be happier if, in a marriage, she continued to have her own circle of friends and hobbies. Not at all because Mark is incapable of love, but, quite simply because a relationship for him is not a top priority at all times. In the home, he would need an emotional supporter, not a rival. Hearing this was a relief to her, as she had been worried that should they become involved, she might not be able to keep up with him.

With great joy, Rachel called me a year later to tell me that she had left the firm to take a permanent job elsewhere and was thrilled when Mark called a week later to ask her out. He had not wanted to mix his personal and professional life, but had certainly noticed her from the beginning and indeed liked her a great deal.

The 8th Secret for Finding Your Perfect Match:

T-bars and Upper Strokes

How can you tell if you are dealing with a dynamic, driven achiever, a more laid-back person, or someone totally lacking all motivation? Although one of the best ways to check ambition levels is through the t-bars, these can change rapidly according to the state of mind of the writer. The direction of the t-bar will only indicate how the writer himself is viewing the progress in both his career and financial life at the present moment.

An active and inquiring business mind will tend to show through in the pressure used to apply the pen or pencil to the paper, which also shows strength of purpose. The speed used to write also indicates a vigor and enthusiasm for life. When the pressure is high, you can feel the impression made by the pencil or pen on the back of the paper. The "upbeat" sample (page 88) shows enthusiasm for life with its fast movement across the page and moderate upward swing of the lines.

Other basic signs of speed are: a definite slope to the right; smooth connected letters; simple letter forms; both the i-dots and the t-bars off to the right of the letter; and no unnecessary starting or ending strokes. Joe Franklin, a pioneer in American talk shows, has very dynamic writing (page 90), as does the television

Upbeat

I live in New York City and my name is Shirley Knight Hopkins

This highly acclaimed actress's writing shows enthusiasm, imagination, and a highly optimistic mood.

news anchor Jim Ryan (see below). Both are in fast moving and highly competitive fields where the ability to think quickly and make instant decisions is vital for survival. Note the high-flying upper loops and t-bars, which are also found in the highly successful television producer's sample (page 91).

Another more subtle way to judge ambition is to see how different a person's script is from the formation of each letter learned at school. Providing that the letter forms are simple in style, then the further away from childhood script, the

Jim Ryan

I live in New York City and my name is Jim Ryan

This Fox TV news anchor's writing shows the leadership qualities illustrated by the high upper and lower loops. Also notice the great attention to detail indicated by the shape and careful positioning of the i dots.

T-bars and Ambition

Very simply put: The higher the bar of the small letter t, the more enthusiastic the writer is feeling about the path of his or her career. This does not necessarily ensure that everything will turn out wonderfully, but rather that the writer is confident.

When the bar is merely horizontal, the writer is not thrilled with the work situation at the moment. Alternatively, he or she may feel that a project just is not turning out well.

With the down-turned bar of a small t, we find someone who is either out of work, hates the current job, or has a financial problem.

Do always remember that the ambition seen through the t-bar is a reflection of the writer's attitude at that moment as should not be thought of as a blanket statement concerning his career thoughts and hopes. These can change very quickly indeed.

more individual the person will be. Bill Bradley's sample (page 93) shows an individual style of letter shapes with the upward swing of speed.

Once again, do bear in mind that what you may look for in a business partner is very different from what you may choose in a life partner. In fact, the entrepreneurial style of writing (high upper loops, high t-bars, speed, and pressure) is the only one, which is not usually best suited to someone with the same attributes. Prince Albert of Monaco's signature (page 91) shows the very high upper levels often found in heads of companies. In his case, it exhibits his natural ability to take on the duties of running his country. These people attract supportive team people, although they are the last ones to think that they need help in any way. If you think of the life of a tycoon, then you may realize that there is an army of assistants behind him. In his personal life, the spouse is more often than not a nurturer rather than another powerhouse.

Joe Franklin

One of the "founding fathers" of radio and television talk shows. Note the high swings of the t-bars and the height of the capital letters and general appearance of speed and vitality in the writing. This is a man always on the go with an amazing memory and zest for life.

Looking at the needs of the nurturer of the highly ambitious person, we find someone who would be happier if there are other close personal relationships to fulfill her greater emotional needs. This is not to say that the ambitious person is not fully capable of loving and caring but that is only a part of his life, by no means all of it. He will always be more involved with his projects than with his home life. To be content in this situation, the

Prince Albert of Monaco

The extremely high upper loops coupled with the high-flying t-bar show a great deal of ambition, business imagination and drive. The shape of the capital M with the second stroke being the highest part of the letter is found in those with a sense of superiority. Very appropriate in a future monarch.

Highly Successful Television Producer

Note the very high upper loops, showing she has all the imagination and creativity needed to work on one of the major morning shows. Note the flying t-bars of ambition

Napoleon Bonaparte

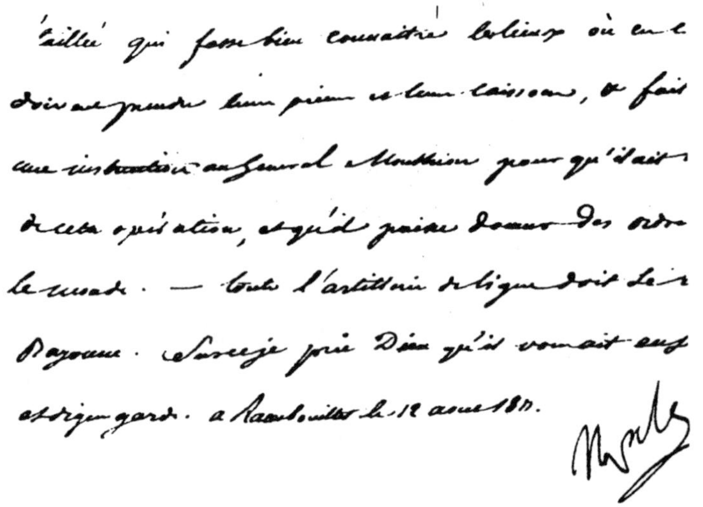

[handwritten letter in French]

The strong surge to the right but without losing any of the neatly placed i-dots tells us of this masterful strategist's drive and attention to detail.

nurturer is happy if she remains involved with extended family and friends to take up what she may perceive as the emotional slack in the relationship.

When identifying the ambitious personality, do not forget that drive on it's own does not always equal success. A down side to the enterprising person can be a restlessness, which may cause boredom before a project is completed. Also, bear in mind that he or she may be very aggressive in moving ahead on a scheme, which will bring no financial reward. Being entrepreneurial does not automatically mean being wealthy.

Few people are highly ambitious. Most of us exist in a more or less happy state of accepting the status quo. That is not to say

Bill Bradley

In Jack
To the Man who
my not have been my
all-time amust leade

VINTAGE BOOKS *Princeton -*

A Division of Random House, Inc.

New York

Bill Bradly

Originally a successful sportsman, he continued to use his ambi-tion in the field of politics.

that they make no effort to improve their situation, but it is not an all-consuming desire. The great majority of people are followers and team players. On the whole, they lead more balanced lives than the highly ambitious people tend to do. This is shown in their handwriting because there are fewer very high upper strokes or very deep lower strokes; they divide their time more evenly between family, friends, and work.

The go-getter, however, is rarely off-duty. Even when enjoying a leisurely Sunday lunch he may see a potential client and cannot resist making contact. He cannot help it—he sees it as almost a crime to let an opportunity slip by. His lunch companion may see it very differently. If the person is already very successful, why spoil lunch to make a little more money? The actual joy of the deal is what counts and the potential money

Babe Ruth

The little hooks in this writing are the signs of great tenacity and strength of will.

is usually a side issue. More often than not, success comes not from the love of money but earning achievements in a chosen field. Financial gain is a pleasant by-product.

Jackie Kennedy exhibited strong leadership qualities in running the domestic tasks in the White House while her husband was in office—even though her skills were employed in a quiet and diplomatic way. Her writing is composed of very high upper loops, indicating the imaginative, ambitious personality (page 95). She very quickly and superbly re-decorated the mansion, which was no small achievement. In the sample of Napoleon's writing (page 92), the rush off to the right (the future) can be clearly seen, but also notice that he exhibits a fine eye for detail shown by the closely dotted *i*'s. He was one of the most ambitious men in history and this script seems to almost charge forward, befitting such a military leader.

A further indication of ambition is found when there are small hooks in the writing. They show that the writer is tenacious, stubborn, and has great determination to complete whatever they set their mind to. Babe Ruth's writing (page 94) is

Jackie Kennedy

I could have these for Inauguration Day so you'll have to rush — sent to Washington —

Thank you
Jacqueline Kennedy

Ambition is shown here in a different manner. The very high upper slopes are typical of an entrepreneurial person, but here they are added to a very left slope and disconnected letters. Put together, these add up to a brilliant researcher. Later in life, she used these talents in her publishing career.

full of the little hooks of tenacity, and he certainly overcame a lot of early setbacks and a difficult childhood to achieve through talent and sheer strength of will.

Exercise 8

You will both need to write out the following words: "I try my best at tests." Look at the direction of the t-bars to see the level of ambition at the moment.

Hers

Chapter 9

Generous or Thrifty?

Jane and Gordon

When Jane arrived for her session, she was loaded down with shopping bags and I could not help but notice that they were all from very expensive stores on Madison Avenue.

Looking first at her handwriting, I saw that it was fairly large and the letters were wide and full of curves, indicating her warmth and generosity. The sample she had brought with her was in complete contrast because it had writing that was very small and narrow, almost pinched in style with no upward curves at the end of the words. This obviously belonged to a person with a much more economical and conservative approach to life than she had.

After I had pointed out this very basic difference in personality types to Jane, she told me that this was the handwriting of Gordon, her new boyfriend of four months. They had found that they enjoyed many of the same things such as films, baseball, hiking, and museums. Jane met him at a baseball game she had gone to with her brother. The two men struck up a conversation and then the three of them went out for coffee after the game.

Since then, they had been seeing each other about two or three times a week and were beginning to think seriously about a future together. One thing that was bothering her very much though, was his attitude to money. When they had started to go out, Jane had thought that Gordon was not doing very well in business. He drove a small, 5-year-old car and lived in a pleasant but fairly modest apartment. He insisted that he pay for all of their entertainment, but always kept to a tight, fixed budget. His idea of a perfect vacation would be a fishing trip at a friend's cottage. Hers was more along the lines of a luxury Caribbean resort.

She had been shocked to find out that he worked in his family firm, in an executive position, and that it was a very successful publishing firm that he stood to inherit in time. He had more than once politely questioned her about her spending habits and now she wondered if he was miserly by nature.

We talked at length about her handling of money and found she was, despite a prosperous appearance, having financial problems. In fact, she had a low-paying job, still lived at home, and she gave her divorced mother very little for rent and food. She spent all her income on clothes and personal items and she was behind on her credit card payments. Buying things, whether she needed them or not, gave her a temporary sense of pleasure and security. Unfortunately, that sense of security did not seem to extend to a more responsible handling of her credit debt.

In working out her issues with Gordon, I told her that his idea of conserving money, although this might seem cheap to her, would in fact ensure a truly secure future for them. If they were to be married and she stopped working to raise a family, she would probably be more happy if they agreed for her to have her own separate bank account. Money would be regularly deposited into the account and she would spend the money as she wished without reporting to Gordon. In this way, they would both feel that they had a certain amount of financial control in the marriage. This is exactly what they agreed upon later.

Despite the fact that they had very opposing ideas about money, with understanding and cooperation, they were able to reach an agreement on domestic financial issues while maintaining a certain amount of their personal attitudes.

The 9th Secret for Finding Your Perfect Match:

Word Endings and Width

As the old saying goes, "money is the root of all evil"—or at least, the cause of many a disagreement. Differing views about money can cause the most loving relationships to flounder, so take much care here. Generosity in a love partner may be initially desired, but viewed with more caution in a marriage partner, particularly if money is short. On the other hand, a thrifty attitude in a new partner may not be very attractive, but might be a desirable approach in a marriage.

In planning a future together with someone, the long-term goals are often very different from the early dating stages. Evenings out, for example, are a usual start to a romance and both partners may spend more than they can comfortably afford. At this time, when

Generosity/Thriftiness

"nothing is too much to give you"

Wide writing with little upward curves on the letter endings equal a generous nature.

"I don't believe in extravagance"

Pinched writing with sharp letter endings indicate a frugal position.

"I love to acquire, grab and hoard things"

Notice the hook of the letter g; this is a "money hook" of someone who collects things for him- or herself.

both people may be trying to impress the other, it is useful to have insights into the true financial personality of your potential partner.

Further into a relationship, we start to see our partner's financial patterns. In life, many people find other people's economies and strategies strange—the shopoholic who nevertheless saves every piece of string, or the retired person who lives on Social Security, doesn't eat enough, but lavishes gourmet food on his dog.

Frugal

Dear Sirs,
I would like to inform you that I will be in London on June 1st, unless I cannot make it in time, in that case I will telephone you before coming.
I remain yours for ever,

Yours faithfully

The pinched, tight-looking letters indicate a person of very thrifty habits.

In considering the future, the person who is thoughtful in providing for older parents will undoubtedly be a good provider for children. That same person may seem to you to be overly economic in choosing a restaurant and carefully going over the bill, but will have a savings plan for those children's education.

The two main parts of handwriting that illustrate the degree of generosity are the word endings and the width of the writing. These indicate generosity of spirit as well as financial generosity. If you should notice that at the end of each word there are not little upward swings, but rather an abrupt end, then you are looking at the writing of someone who is frugal by nature. If in addition to the sharp word endings you notice that the writing is very narrow and rather pinched looking, your partner is literally "penny-pinching." The sample "frugal" (above) shows the very narrow writing of a very cheap person.

Alternatively, if his writing is wide and full and has pleasant upswings at the end of words, he is warm and giving by nature. The "warm and generous" sample (page 102) shows these characteristics.

Warm and Generous

I live in New York City and my name is

The broad writing and upswings of the end strokes tell of a benevolent nature.

The "thrift" sample (page 103) has an absence of curves at the end of his words, which are cut off rather sharply. This person has a great reluctance to part with his money and constantly tries to bargain with his debtors to pay back outstanding amounts little by little. Another aspect found in handwriting, although rarely, is called the "money claw." If you look at the sample "prison inmate" (page 103), you will see that there are several of the lower loops of the *g*'s and *y*'s with a claw, or hook, at the bottom. This is found in people whose main emphasis in life is acquiring money or valuable items. As the name 'money claw' implies, this is not the most attractive personality trait, exhibiting a very grasping nature.

Prison Inmate

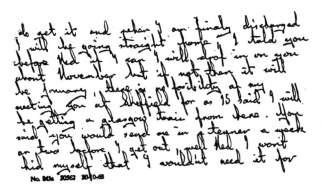

No. 843a 305612 30-10-68

The money hooks underneath the small g's and y's throughout this note (not to mention the actual request for cash) shows someone who is deeply interested in acquiring money. In this case, however, not very successfully.

Thrift

Although this letter talks about payment, with the lack of upward swings, plus the very wide spacing, it does not inspire confidence. Although this letter referred, in fact, to a luxury item purchased, it seems that the small amount of money needed had to be transferred to cover the check.

Exercise 9

As always, in script, please write out the following: "Attitudes toward money matter a lot."

Check the ends of the letters *a* and *t* to see if they have curves to the right or not, and also if the letters are fairly broad or very narrow.

His

Hers

Chapter 10

Logical or Intuitive?

Beth, Ben, and Sam

When Beth made her appointment to see me, she told me that she was looking for an assessment of her two teenage boys, Ben and Sam. She told me that she was in her mid-30s and had been married since she was 21. Her boys were now 14 and 15 years old.

When she arrived to see me, Beth showed me the samples of her own handwriting and that of both of the boys'. I noticed that in both her writing and in Ben's, the letters in each word were joined to the next letter. There were no gaps left in between. Most people do have this connected writing indicating what is called the "logical problem-solving process." They do tend to think things through in a logical progression and come to conclusions having weighed the facts.

Sam's writing, however, was almost entirely disconnected, meaning that each letter in each word stood by itself, without being attached to it's neighboring letters. This indicates what is known as the "intuitive problem solving process." Sam gathers his information from many different sources. Such people are very open to ideas and people and are much influenced by their surroundings. It can, therefore, be quite difficult for them to concentrate for long periods of time on one subject, as they are constantly receiving so many impressions. In his particular case, I could see that this was modified somewhat by the very precisely dotted small i's, but even so, his mind works a little differently than most people's.

The older boy, Ben, was very much like his mother. They were full of life, social, and hard-working. He consistently earned grades that were a little above average and had little trouble applying himself every night to his homework.

But it was Sam, the 14-year-old, that Beth was concerned about. He was highly intelligent, charming, and had many friends, but his grades were unpredictable. In some subjects he excelled one semester and then dropped off dramatically the next. When asked why he would suddenly fail in a subject he had done well in before, Sam would merely say he was not interested at the moment.

Without meaning to, Sam often annoyed people by having the right answers to questions, but seemed unable to explain how he arrived at that conclusion. His mother and his teachers felt that he was simply not bothering to tell them. This was not true—he really would not know from where he received his information. I explained to Beth that her son would perform the best in subjects that allowed him to use his imagination. Homework was always a challenge because Sam did not seem to be able to concentrate on anything for too long.

Beth had spoken to his teachers and the school counselor, as well as the family doctor, and all had assured her that there was nothing wrong with the boy other than his tendency to daydream. In discussing this problem with Beth, I did ask her if Sam had been clinically assessed, as I always strongly urge people to consult with medical professionals about anything that could be attributed to a physical or psychological problem. If no evidence of such a problem is found, then handwriting analysis is a very valuable tool.

I wanted Beth to realize that Sam was not trying to be difficult and that it was likely that he would only do well in subjects that captured his imagination. I was not suggesting that she stop encouraging him with his school work, but told her that many times he would be unable to do long stints of homework in the same manner as his more disciplined brother. He was not lazy, but his mind operated in a rather different way than the majority of people.

A few years later, Beth told me that Sam had started to excel in science and was spending long hours in the lab experimenting. It seemed that at last he had found something that was varied enough to stimulate him and he was doing remarkably well. Beth was relieved that his particular talents had found a positive outlet.

The 10th Secret for Finding Your Perfect Match:

Joined Letters

What factors indicate if a person is basically intuitive or logical in their approach to life? This shows up in writing by whether the letters in a word are all joined to each other, or if there are spaces

Robert Muller

To Bryce Boud

May we all help

the hopes of humanity

Come true

21 Nov. 1985   Robert Muller

The totally disconnected writing speaks of a highly intuitive mind.

between them. If there is a constant train of thought and the ability to concentrate, then the letters are connected to one another. If there are breaks between the letters, there are also breaks in concentration as is found in the intuitive, creative, and easily distracted mind.

It may interest you to know that when this difference was first observed very many years ago, that it was also noted that far more women than men have the disconnected, intuitive style of writing. This is also the reason why women are far more capable than men of performing multiple tasks simultaneously. Most men are at their best concentrating their attention entirely on one thing at a time.

Disconnected

Dear Fellow Pilgrims!

I hope your re-entry to the modern world wasn't too jarring. I expect, like me, you are still digesting fragments of memories of scenes of places we visited —so many and so rich!

This writing belongs to someone whose life's work is devoted to esoteric discoveries.

The instinctual person may not realize that they are "playing hunches" a lot of the time, but indeed their minds are constantly bombarded with input. They have the ability to think about several different things at once. Concentration on one subject at a time can be very difficult and school may be a problem. The lack of concentration has nothing to do with IQ, but rather with the multitude of ideas crowding the mind. With all of that brain activity, it can be extremely difficult to pay attention to a teacher for very long.

Many brilliant people have disconnected writing and did not flourish within the structure of formal education, but blossomed later when they were able to set their own pace. The writer Robert Muller's book inscription (page 108) shows very disconnected writing. Muller's handwriting can be compared to the sample "disconnected" (above).

The logical problem-solving partner tends to believe that his ideas are more sound and well-argued, having been carefully thought out. One could think of it as almost a chain reaction leading to a conclusion. So when a logical person encounters an intuitive person, who comes out with an apparently off the cuff brilliant idea, it is particularly annoying because it appears to have no basis in reason. President Jimmy Carter

Jimmy Carter

This almost totally disconnected writing belongs to someone whose mind is both full of many ideas at the same time and makes fast and accurate decisions by pure instinct.

(right) and the writer Kenneth Graham (page 111) both have disconnected writing, but in each case it has been modified with a closely dotted small *i*. This adds a degree of attention to detail, in what would otherwise have been a "butterfly mind" (one that alights briefly upon too many different subjects, but not staying long enough to acquire any real knowledge).

The samples of Bruce Springsteen (page 112) and Leslie Flint (page 113) show highly intuitive people, although they have used their ability in very different ways. Bruce Springsteen writes music, which speaks to so many people. Leslie Flint had an unparalleled ability to communicate with the spirit world.

This is one aspect reflected in handwriting that shows a personality that can be irritating to the opposite type. If you are the logical, problem-solving type and are dealing with the intuitive problem-solving person who (truthfully) tells you that he has "no

Kenneth Graham

Dear Robinson

The Water-Rat put out a neat little brown paw, + gave Toady a big hoist + a pull, over the edge of the hole, + there was Mr. Toad at last, standing safe + sound in the hall, covered with mud, + with the water streaming off him, but pleased +

Notice the letters are not all connected to each other. The author of Wind in the Willows *seems to have been inspired to dream up his wonderful characters without his ever really knowing where they came from.*

idea" how he arrived at a correct conclusion, you may not believe him. You may also believe that he is too lazy to bother to explain his reasoning to you. This is not so. Why? Because the person who writes with space between the letters of their words really does gather information from many different sources and they usually do not remember from where. The people who write with all the letters connected find this very difficult to understand because they are more methodical and would also know how they came to a conclusion.

Merely because a person has disconnected writing does not in itself prove that the person has unusual ESP or is totally illogical.

Nor should the person with completely connected letters be presumed to have absolutely no intuitive abilities. We all do to some extent, but it is a question of degree.

There is no way either person can learn how to change this trait. If two partners have these two differing characteristics, it is usually somewhat annoying, but not a catastrophic problem in a relationship.

Bruce Springsteen

With a mixture of high upper loops (inspiration) and very disconnected letters, this highly accomplished musician obviously draws very much upon his intuition for his work.

Leslie Flint

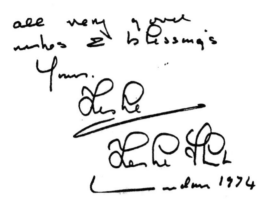

This very disconnected writing belongs to the uniquely gifted direct-voice medium, who had exceptional intuitive powers.

Exercise 10

In cursive writing, both you and your partner need to write the following words: "Am I a logical or an intuitive person?"

Whether or not the letters are connected to one another will give you the answer.

Hers

Chapter 11

Detailed or Casual?

Herbert and his employees

A year ago, Herbert had realized his dream of opening his own public relations firm. He was highly creative, and although his thoughts were scattered, his clients loved his spontaneity and quick wit. His mother had always said he would lose his head if it was not attached, but somehow he always managed to produce his work on time.

The reason that he came to see me was that he was having a lot of trouble with the selection of staff for his new office. Not with the creative team, who reacted positively to his style and flair, but with the administrative people. He had sent over a folder full of handwriting samples of past and present employees prior to our meeting.

When I reviewed these with him a week later, I told him that I could see immediately what the problem was. He had chosen each one of them, regardless of job function, with the characteristics he would look for in a friend. It is quite understandable that when someone first opens his own business, he might like to feel that everyone is his buddy, but in any office environment, a variety of attributes is needed. Given Herbert's own complete lack of organization, a whole company of people like him would produce chaos in no time at all.

We discussed at some length what qualities he required, for example, from the accounting staff. These qualities would not be the same as what he should look for in his personal assistant. This does not mean to say that he should be forced to employ people he did not like, but that he had to think in terms of being the boss, not everyone's friend. After all, he did have a wife, children, and social life outside the office.

In helping him select a financial planner, we took from a pile of applications the one whose writing showed superb organizational skills. The man's use of the page reflected his ability to prioritize work projects. The letter formation was neat and there was an even space on both the left and right margin. With similar spaces at the top and bottom of the page, it almost looked as if it had been typed out.

Herbert's own writing was as chaotic as his personality. His enthusiastic bursts often took his writing crashing into the right-hand side of the page. The letters at the top of the page were very large but by the end of the page, as he was running out of space, they became much smaller. Without the quiet efficiency of the new financial person and his personal assistant, he would have drowned in the complete confusion around him. Frankly, he found his assistant a little dull, but after all, she was not there to amuse him, but to organize his office.

Over a period of time he learned to let his accounting and administrative staff get on with their work, while being able to share his excitement over new projects with the creative team.

He also learned to respect other people's ability to prioritize and execute work in a timely fashion, without which the firm would not have survived. He was now surrounded by people whose abilities complemented his own. As a result of the improved efficiency in the office, Herbert found that he had more time to spend with his family and friends.

The 11th Secret for Finding Your Perfect Match:

Layout and I-dots

How important are details to you? This can be a major issue in all relationships. If one person is extremely precise and detail-oriented, this may strike another type of person as nitpicky and very restricting. The other end of the spectrum is the more bohemian lifestyle, lacking many of the formalities of housekeeping—this can be very annoying to a person who likes routine and order.

How many times have you laughed when you heard that people separated because they had different ways of squeezing the toothpaste tube? The non-conformist personality tends not to mix well with the meticulous traits of the orderly types. We all know people who seem to lurch from one crisis to another, permanently in chaos. This is deeply frustrating to a partner who is trying to bring order and tranquillity to their situation. As it will not happen, extraordinary tolerance is needed from the more organized partner. This is not a question of right or wrong, merely compatibility.

Details

"I am entirely absorbed with details"

Every i-dot is in perfect place just above the body of the letter and every t-bar is the same length in front and behind the upstroke of the letter.

"Sometimes I care about details, sometimes I don't"

A mixture of missing i-dots and crossed and uncrossed t-bars indicate an erratic person.

"What are details?"

When little attention is paid to the correct differences in sizes of capital and small letters, then little attention is being paid to much else either.

In a marriage, we will often find an overworked spouse with a much more domesticated partner. This is not to say that working long hours automatically prevents someone from being tidy at home, but a lack of time can make this a problem. It is obviously important for both people's well-being that they understand that neither is taking the other for granted in this situation and perhaps chores could be shared on the weekends, for example.

The dots of the small *i* and *j* are the best way to observe attention to detail. The closer the dot is to the stem of the letter, the more organized the writer. To put in the i-dot, the writer has to stop and go back to the letter; how carefully this is done shows how carefully he attends to all areas of his life. You will not find a competent financial advisor neglecting to dot his *i*'s.

Sometimes you see writing where some dots are in place and some are either missing or far way. This indicates that the person can apply attention to detail when he wants to—which is not all of the time! Completely missing dots indicates a person who zips through many tasks each day and hopes someone else catches the errors. The driven executive type might not show much attention to the day-to-day routines of the office, but is likely to believe that others will take care of them. In a domestic set-up, the same dynamics will apply, so there will be an over-worked spouse with a more domesticated partner.

How organized you are in all areas of your life is reflected in how you approach a blank piece of paper. A fresh, clean, unlined piece of paper and how you make use of the space will show many things about you, from your aesthetic sense to your feel-ings of economy. Starting with the margins at the top, then the bottom, and finally at both sides, we can see the attitude to the past and the future. The more evenly sized the margins are at the top and bottom, as well as the left and the right, the more mature and balanced the writer is. The sample "page layout" (page 120) shows a good use of space.

The left-hand margin represents the past, the one that is being left behind as we write. It is very rare to see a page of writ-ing that does not have this left margin. When the left margin is very narrow, the person is holding onto the comfort level asso-ciated with people and things from the past; they are nervous about new situations and relationships. Partnerships by their very nature tear us away from our former life, and this can pro-duce anxiety. In looking at the left-hand margin, be aware that if someone is writing very quickly, it is normal that this margin gets wider as the page goes on. On the other hand, if you see that your partner's writing gets closer and closer to the left, he is slowing down and showing that he is very cautious by nature.

Page Layout

CANADA'S NATIONAL NEWSPAPER

THE GLOBE AND MAIL

Thanks again for
the interview &
the reading / analysis.
And good luck with
your book launch.

Alexandre

444 Front Street West, Toronto Ontario M5V 2S9

This sample shows a very good aesthetic sense of placement of words on the page.

The right-hand margin is where all writing, and life itself, is going. The more we are open to change, the more comfortable we are in allowing our words to be near this side of the paper. Even if it is narrow, there must always be a margin. A very wide margin on the right indicates a person who is fearful of the future. If you see that the writing collides with the right-hand side of the page, there is almost too much enthusiasm to move forward.

Top and bottom margins, apart from the overall sense of balance they give to a page of writing, have less psychological meanings. Traditionally, the top margin was said to show the

Organization

Two very different samples; the first is a person filling all possible areas of the page and, therefore, her life. The second example is of someone who is very anxious about the future (the right side of the page) and goes to extremes to avoid it.

degree of respect the writer was showing toward the addressee. The wider the margin, the greater the respect.

Very evenly sized top, bottom, and side margins show excellent organization in life. The way in which Madonna's note (page 122) is laid out is a superb example of organization, but it might almost have been composed on a computer. In the sample "organization," (above), we see two very different people. The first is overly anxious to fill up the page (and her life). The second is manifesting great anxiety about the future and is trying hard to hold onto the past.

Rockwell Kent's sense of detail is obvious (page 123). Much of his work was devoted to engravings where making a mistake is not an option. Incidentally, his actual writing (this is much enlarged to be at all legible) is the smallest I have ever seen and needs a magnifying glass to be read. In the sample "attention to detail" (page 123), these three handwriting samples belong to accountants. Each one has closely dotted *i*'s and small but very precise letter formation.

In both Sir Arthur Conan Doyle and Dane Rhudyar's writing you will see very neat i-dots (page 124). The closer the dot is to the stem of the writing, the more precise in all areas of life is the writer. When you first look at the sample of Charles Dickens (page 125), it looks like a complete mess, but look more carefully. Remember this was written long before typewriters or computers were invented. Now you will see that all the i-dots are in the correct place.

Madonna

The attention to layout shown in this note for a video shoot tells us of the organization and great attention to detail for which this driven media star is so well known.

On the other hand, the "muddled" sample (page 125) is exactly that—a perfect example of the writing of a very confused person.

Rockwell Kent

What do you regard as your distinctive or characteristic technical
method or achievement?

I am a realist ; and in the vision of the Almighty. I amal
make this vision and am a thing imagined but - being seen an
With all good wishes to yourself, I am,

Faithfully yours,

Rockwell Kent

RK sj   Rockwell Kent

This celebrated artist was known for many types of work but
also excelled in engravings and graphic art. This sample was
much magnified as the original is so tiny that it is hardly legible.
It is an extreme specimen of precision.

Attention to Detail

I live in New York City and my name is

I live in New York and
my name is

I live in New York City
and my name is

Three samples, all showing a very fine eye for details with closely
dotted i's and very careful letterform.

Sir Arthur Conan Doyle

Notice the very carefully formed letters and the appearance of speed, but without missing any i-dots. There is a general thoroughness about the presentation of this letter. But what else would you expect from the author of that most logical of men, Sherlock Holmes?

Dane Rhudhyar

This eminent astrologer's writing, with the small letters and carefully dotted i's illustrates perfectly the fine attention to detail needed in the calculation of natal charts.

Muddled

The frequent corrections and erasures on this note show little flow of thought.

Charles Dickens

Today it is hard to imagine that this scribbled mess was the beginning of A Christmas Carol, *but do not forget that this was in the days long before computers. In this case, the sense of organisation was without fault.*

Exercise 11

This exercise requires you both to write: "I am wondering if I am orderly and precise or more casual in style?"

First, see if all of the *i*'s have been dotted. Then observe how the words have been placed in the space available to them.

His

Hers

Chapter 12

Signatures

Christine and her names

Christine is a successful soap opera star in her early 30s. She had briefly been married when she was very young and had taken her husband's name. In choosing a name for her theatrical career, she had decided to take her grandmother's maiden name.

When she came to see me, she was about to remarry and had questions about the variety of names she was, and would be, using. As it was, whenever she was asked to sign anything, she tended to hesitate and had to remind herself of which persona she was adopting at the moment. This was becoming confusing.

Her own maiden name was, of course, the one she felt was truly her own and she still used it from time to time. Her married name belonged to a man she hardly chose to remember at this time in her life. She had been very attached to her grandmother and felt that changing her stage name would not be possible, nor did she want to change it. On top of all this, she would now legally have the right to use the name of her second husband, if she wished to.

I asked her to write out all of the signatures on one piece of paper—her maiden name, her first married name, her stage name, and finally, her to-be newly married name. I also asked her to write out a few lines of script before I could truly comment on the signatures. The reason I asked for all of the samples is because a person's writing tells who she truly is and the signature tells us how she would like to be seen by the world in general. How a person genuinely is and how she projects herself are not always the same.

As I have found in many actors, Christine's writing was fairly small and sloped to the left. One might imagine that all theatrical people would have large, flamboyant writing with a distinct right slope, but that it not always so. Christine's style was modest and analytical—a person who brings unusual depth to her performances. Although her work at the moment was on a soap opera, her background was on the stage performing the classics. As I expected, her signatures were all quite different, larger than the writing, and quite bold in style.

The initial *C* of Christine was the largest letter of all in the four signatures and that told me that she felt she had achieved everything very much by herself. The manner in which she had written the surname of her first husband was highly revealing; even the capital letter of the name was very small and the rest of the name was scrawled and illegible. She had no respect for him and was in many ways canceling him out.

Her stage name, using her grandmother's maiden name, had both initial letters written in a large and clear style. She had much admiration and love for the lady. Her maiden name was, again, written fairly clearly, but not as boldly as her stage name. The surname, a reflection of her father because it was his name, was legible and well formed, revealing a good relationship with him.

The final signature was that which included her financé's name and in this, both her initial *C* and the initial letter of his family name were of equal size. I felt she was entering this marriage with a feeling of love and equality. On summing up these signatures, she decided that from now on she would only be using her stage name and newly married name, thereby putting the past behind her.

The 12th Secret for Finding Your Perfect Match:

Signatures

Your signature will always be the most important thing you ever write. In ancient times, everything that was written was so precious that even illiterates had to scratch an X to represent themselves. Over the centuries, this has evolved into each of us having a unique signature by which we are known. It is as personal to you as your fingerprint or DNA. Only fingerprints equal an autograph when considering ease and accuracy in making an identification.

We must always take the bulk of the handwriting as reflecting the complete, true personality of the person we are studying because the signature alone cannot be used to reveal the full personality. Rather, the signature will tell you how your partner is projecting himself to the world in general (the ego statement) and how he would like to be seen by others. When we can see that the style of the handwriting and the signature are exactly the same, we can say with complete confidence that the person is absolutely the same as the way they present themselves. Many times, though, this is not the case.

It is also quite common for people to use one type of signature for business and another for personal correspondence. Many married women today use both their maiden and married names; sometimes together, sometimes one or the other, depending on the occasion for writing.

We may find a modest, studious type hiding behind a hugely theatrical signature. Does this mean a deliberately false impression? No. It's just a subconscious smoke screen. We can also never tell whether a person will grow into the different personality shown by a varying signature. The future cannot be seen in a person's handwriting, although the potential certainly can.

The signature will tell you a great deal about the person's childhood and how it has been dealt with. If the first name is written out in full (and clearly), this indicates that the social and economic situations of the early childhood have been accepted. Not necessarily liked or disliked, but not a problem which needs to be suppressed. On the other hand, if the first name is either not written in full or is illegible, then the issues of early childhood remain unresolved.

The size of the signature compared to the letter is very significant. If it is mostly the same, the person is at terms with himself. A very large first letter of the first name tells us that the writer truly feels that he has done everything for himself and therefore, he owes no one else anything for his achievements (this may or may not be so, but it is the true perception of the writer).

Signatures

In **Jimmy Carter's** *signature, the enlarged* C *shows great respect for his father. Mrs. Carter's enlarged* C *shows her respect for her husband.*

Hillary Rodham Clinton's *signature shows three different things. The enlarged* H *shows that she believes she has achieved everything by herself. The enlarged* R *indicates respect for her father. Finally, the comparatively small* C *indicates that her respect for her husband is quite a bit lower than her self-respect.*

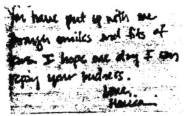

President **Bill Clinton's** *and* **Monica Lewinsky's** *signatures are somewhat similar in style. Both are a little off to the left, in the middle zone of materialism. A basic difference is seen in the final* a *of Monica. This long line to the right from this letter shows an uncomfortable person socially, who overextends herself to other people and then wishes she had not.*

In a man's signature, the family name will tell us how he views his father. In a woman's signature, the family name could be one of three people: father, husband, or ex-husband. It will reveal her view of that man. When there has been an unhappy life with a father or husband, his name will show very different aspects than the rest of the writing. In either sex, when the first letter of the family name is written very much larger that the capital of the writer's first name, then he or she has great respect for the father's (or husband's) achievements. This does not imply affection, or not, just respect.

Unless it is on a very casual note, signing with only one initial is not the best impression a person could give of himself. That would literally be diminishing yourself! Also, although fairly rare, you will see that the first capital letter of the given name is written in small form. Although this is sometimes a deliberate artistic gesture, it is more often a sign of insecurity and feelings of inferiority.

Many people draw a line under their signature; this is a mixture of caution and self-confidence. When your loved one draws a line above his name, he is keeping the world from getting too close to him and he will take a long time to open up to you. A person attempting to shield himself from harm writes a signature with a circle all the way around it.

When looking for a partner, there is one little clue that will give you great insight into how they thought of you at the time of writing. Simply—have they written your name larger than their own? If so—terrific! If your name is much smaller, then so are you in their eyes.

Signatures

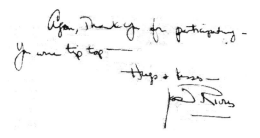

Joan Rivers: *Looking carefully at the final letter of the first name, you will see that it slopes back over with a small hook at the end. Despite a sometimes cutting wit, this comedienne is very self-protective and more vulnerable than would appear.*

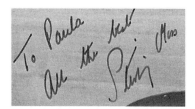

Stirling Moss: *The extremely enlarged S of the first name is the best indication of the person who absolutely believes that he has made his own way in life and owes no one else for his racing success.*

Boris Karloff: *The letterform of this signature is angular, indicating someone who could be very demanding.*

Signatures

Charlie Chaplin signature

Charlie Chaplin: *With its very obvious right slope, his signature shows a huge enthusiasm for life. However, notice that each letter is quite clear. He is fast, but also accurate.*

Don Johnson signature

Don Johnson's *complex signature with the almost complete encircling of the first name by the second shows a person hiding a very private face behind his achievements.*

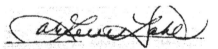

Arlene Dahl's *signature is fascinating because there is such a mixture of flamboyance and reserve. The large embellished letters almost conceal the small capital A of Arlene. It is most unusual for the first name to be written in the diminutive form, showing shyness.*

Quentin Crisp signature

Quentin Crisp's *unique brand of wit is seen in the little circle instead of a dot on top of the i of Crisp.*

Signatures

Colette's strength of will and tenacity is seen in the hook at the very end of her name. It is also directed back at herself, showing how critical she could be of herself. The t-bar above the body of the letter tells us that she was in a highly creative mode at the time this was written and had a project in mind.

Out of the writers shown here, **Stephen King**'s is the most complex. The huge lasso effect above his first name means two things. First, a desire to keep everyone away. Second, in traditional graphology, it would have been said that he enjoyed crossword puzzles. In this day and age, one would say he enjoys mind games.

Carl Jung's signature is a mixture of the high upper loops of inspiration and imagination, and full left-wing lower loops which show his repsect for family and tradition. The connecting line between the C and G indicate an interesting desire that no one look too closely at his own early family life.

Signatures

Astrud Gilberto's signature, with the much larger A than G, shows a person who believes that she has made her own way in

Rae Dawn Chong's signature has all the self-confidence and flair needed to be a film star.

Chris Noth's signature is larger than life, as are many of the acting parts he has chosen. However, notice the disconnected letters in the word "Noth." This means that he brings a very intuitive part to his roles.

Cyndi Lauper's signature is very much off to the left, but with large capital letters. This is a very private person who has a great ability to perform when she so chooses.

Signatures

Marc Chagall: *This celebrated artist's signature is surprisingly clear and precise in the letterform. This means that he wished to be seen for exactly who he was.*

Barbara Hepworth: *This strong, arcade-style signature is a reflection of the powerful work by this British sculptor. Also not the flying t-bar which is a great sign of ambition.*

Gloria Vanderbilt Cooper: *The much larger G of the first name tells us that this accomplished lady feels that she has done a lot entirely for herself.*

Exercise 12

In this final exercise, write out this sentence and follow it with your regular signature: "I believe that the personality shown in my signature truly reflects me."

Check to see if the style and size of the sentence is the same as the signature.

His

Chapter 13

Doodles

Caren and Lenny

Caren was worried when she noticed that Lenny's desk pad was scrawled over and over with dollar signs and both his and her names. Also, there were arrows all around the dollar signs. What could this mean?

My interpretation of the doodles was, because they had been discussing marriage, Lenny was putting a great deal of energy (arrows) into his work as a stockbroker (by nature, a highly competitive, aggressive field). His motivation (dollar signs) was to have enough money to buy a house for their new life together.

Writing of one's own and one's partner's name over and over again is a delightful, almost childish way of reinforcing the idea of their union. Caren was much relieved to learn that the doodles were an entirely innocent display of his sincerity toward her and their marriage.

Gary and Lorraine

Gary had felt almost guilty about bringing me four sheets of Lorraine's doodles, as he had not told her that he had taken them,

Caren and Lenny

Lenny's doodles of dollar signs with arrows and the repeating of Caren and his names over and over symbolized his energy going into making money for their future and his commitment to the relationship.

and felt that doodles are particularly private. The reason that he had sought my advice was that their engagement had just been announced and since then he had noticed that she had seemed rather cool toward him. He was hoping that he was not making a mistake.

Lorraine's page of doodles were full of little houses—usually a very benign aspect—except that here they were all enclosed by thick black lines boxing in the houses. Not only that, but there were large black X's scratched through each one of them.

I asked Gary if he thought that Lorraine was truly happy about any plans they had to move when they got married. He told me that he had decided they would go out to the suburbs (where she knew no one) and start a family fairly soon. He admitted that this was his idea and that she had not said much about it. He knew she enjoyed her work, family, and friends, but had thought that their having a new house and children would be a higher priority.

I suggested that he might go back and talk this over with her and, when he did, he found that she was very fearful of the thought of being so isolated. The very fact that she had constantly drawn crossed-out houses showed very clearly how she felt about a move. They decided to compromise and agreed ini-

Loraine and Gary

Lorraine's doodles of houses boxed in by heavy lines and then crossed through, was a subconscious response to her nervousness about moving away from friends and family.

tially on an apartment not so very far from her family, but a little outside the center of town. It would be large enough to start a family in, with the plan that they might move further out into a house in a few years time. Lorraine's doodles had very literally shown the area of her anxiety, which made dealing with it fairly simple.

The 13th Secret for Finding Your Perfect Match:

Doodles

Doodles, those seemingly thoughtless squiggles and symbols made while passing the time at a meeting, or on the phone, reveal

Doodles

Friendly doodles: Flowers, plants, and hearts are all considered to be indications of a contented person.

JFK: A brilliant example in a doodle of the conflicts he was experiencing in his life. The boxing in of any words indicates a great feeling of restriction. Even the boat, although showing a means to freedom, is made up of arrowhead shapes of aggression, as is the triangular doodle.

as much about us as almost anything else we write. The artist Saul Steinberg called them "the brooding of the hand."

Most people doodle and they tend to repeat the same type of doodle. There are several basic styles of doodling: faces, flowers, trees, houses, boxes, spirals, animals, hearts, s-shapes, arrows, signature, and graphic shapes. In basic terms, the doodles that are made of soft shapes and circles are drawn by gentle people. Aggressive personality types draw doodles with sharp angles and points. The intensity of the mood of the moment is shown by

Doodles

Sun, moon, and stars: Heavenly bodies are frequently found in doodles of people with high imagination and thoughts which go far beyond their own personal experiences.

S-shapes, circles, and angles: All of the above are some of the more frequently found doodles. The s-shape is one of the easier to draw while the angular shapes take a little more attention. All of these are considered neutral.

how much pressure is exerted upon the paper and how much the doodle's shape has been filled in. For example, a lightly penned doodle shows a quiet state of mind.

Occasionally you'll see a doodle that has a few words written on it; if you notice that one particular word has a heavy ring around it, you can be sure that it is very significant to the writer. Before you rush to judge your partner based on one or two doodles, make sure you know under what circumstances they were made. For example, if a doodle was made during a telephone argument with his boss, it might show a level of anger that does not apply to all relationships.

Doodles

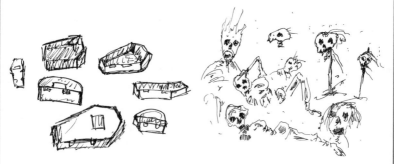

Very worrying doodles: It almost goes without saying that if a person's doodles are made up of caskets and dead people, he is to be viewed with extreme caution!

Problem doodles: Any type of knife, dagger, or sword is an extremely aggressive sign, as are the hearts when they are not only pierced, but obviously bleeding.

Kurt Cobain: *The pain shown in this mangled heart needs no explanation.*

Doodles

*Severe depression: Notice the words "suicidal," "depressions,"
"health," and "mood" are all ringed round and round. Any words
which are so surrounded, should be paid great attention to. Not
because, as is the case here, that there is a problem, but because
those words have great significance to the doodler.*

John Lennon: *An example of his amusing artwork with a doodle of a beetle.*

Doodles

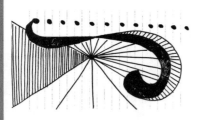

These complex doodles were both done by successful financial people. Both show panning, unusual shapes, and deliberate and purposeful shading.

Two essentially happy doodles: The first is a very naïve form, but smiling. The second is more artistic in style, but also notice that the bird is smiling. Most doodles of animals are benign in meaning, unless the animal is drawn in an obviously aggressive style.

Classic full tree doodle: This indicates a sense of fulfillment in life. The fuller the tree looks, the more content with life the doodler is.

Doodles

Stevie Nicks: *This complex doodle reflects very differing parts of this singer's personality. The round face is typically a friendly doodle, but the rest of the figure has many sharp points of aggression in it and the heart under the name is cut in two.*

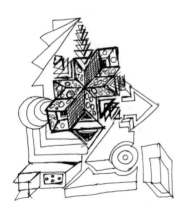

Hillary Rodham Clinton: *A classic example of the complex mind of a strategist.*

Mark Kostabi: *A page as interestingly laid out as one would expect from such a unique artist.*

Doodles

Friendly doodles: Happy faces are all as innocent as they seem.

Houses: Houses are a very common doodle and give insight into the doodler's perception of home. All of the above would be considered very favorable.

Summary

A final word about trying to determine whether or not someone might be your perfect partner in life. The simple answer is that there is no one magic tool to ensure happiness in life, but this book might help you bypass some problems. By looking at someone's handwriting, you can easily see a potential partner's traits and possibilities. Remember, however, that even if they all seem to be entirely agreeable to you, this may be a person with whom you are in sympathy, but this information alone does not guarantee love.

This book started out by asking you to determine if you and your loved one are basically "people" people or more analytical and independent by nature. Most people tend to choose a partner in life who relates in the same way they do to other people.

From there we moved on to considering the balance of ideals, emotions, and everyday material life in our partners and ourselves. This is something we can often allow a fair degree of difference in without being too uncomfortable about it.

An example of a trait we usually have to share with a loved one is whether a person likes to spend most of his time being alone, or is more gregarious. If there is a great difference in the two people's needs, there is likely to be a feeling of neglect by the more sociable partner.

In the chapter concerning modesty and flamboyance, it can be seen that many times opposites do indeed attract, with great success. In fact, two theatrical types may not welcome the competition between them for the limelight.

When looking at the stability of a loved one's moods, great attention must be taken. If fundamental differences are found here, it can quickly cause a relationship to flounder. At the very least, much sympathy and patience is needed if one person is a steady type and the other much more volatile.

Being secretive or open with your feelings are character traits that can be overlooked by many people, if they understand that the differences are not personally directed toward them. The more open and trusting person is never going to see why the secretive person hides so much—each party needs to learn to accept this.

In making a choice of a life partner, the ambition level is often a primary issue to take into account. If both people are driven to success, this can make for a challenging and exciting life. Alternatively, if neither person is motivated to achieve, this can produce problems if there is an accompanying shortage of money. Another type of bonding is found in a highly ambitious person who chooses as a life partner a more domesticated, supportive person to provide balance and tranquillity at home. In these modern days the gender can be either way around.

Money is always an issue in a relationship and how a person deals with money is something that should never be overlooked. Compatibility or resentment in a marriage is often due to the attitude the two people have towards money. In the courtship phase, both people should pay great attention to the other's financial habits.

A common, although fairly minor difference between people is whether one person thinks things through in a logical progression whereas the other is more intuitive in problem solving. Differences here can cause irritation, but are rarely a stumbling block to a relationship.

Whether someone is organized or not can be a pivotal point in a committed relationship. If one person is neat, tidy, and organized but the other is, frankly, a slob, that is problem that must be confronted every single day. Disorganized people who are perpetually in a muddle are a source of great frustration to their more methodical loved ones. Chaotic people often believe that the very things so important to the disciplined partner are in fact trivial and restricting. It is usually hard for these very different types of people to find a way to compromise with each other when they are living together.

The way someone signs his name will tell you a lot about how he presents himself to the world. Also, you can see if this public face reflects the real man.

Doodles tap into the deepest levels of a person. Far from being little squiggles, they are a reflection on the inner person.

This book has attempted to show you an easy way to pick out the personality traits you either like, or think you could live with and also to help you define those traits you do not wish to deal with. After that, one can only wish you the very best of luck in finding that one true love to spend your life with.

Summary Cheat Sheet

1. Check to see in which direction the writing slopes. This is the basic way to see how someone gets on with other people.

2. Are the upper and lower loops the same size as the small letters? If so, it shows a balance between ideals, emotions, and materialism.

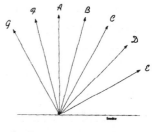

3. Look at the shape of the letters, particularly the small *m* and *n* as a second indicator of how a person interacts with others.

4. See if there is more, or less, space than that of one letter between the words. Much more space shows remoteness, much less shows lack of discrimination.

5. Are the words unusually large, perhaps with many flourishes, showing flamboyance, or unusually small, showing modesty?

6. With a line drawn under the writing, see if it goes straight across the page, or noticeable up or down, showing mood swings.

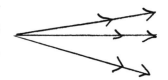

7. Look carefully at the tops of the small *a*'s and *o*'s to see if they are open or tightly closed, as this will tell you how open or secretive a person is.

8. By looking at how high, or low, the bar of the small *t* is written, you can see how ambitious a person is feeling at this time.

9. Generosity is found in the width of each letter and the curves at the end of words. Thriftiness is seen in very narrow writing with abrupt word endings.

10. If the writing has all the letters joined to each other, the person is logical by nature. If the letters are disconnected, then the problem solving process is intuitive.

11. Organization is seen both in the dotting of the small *i* and how the writing is arranged on the page.

12. Finally, does the signature match the style of the writing? If so, the person is projecting exactly who he is.

$\mathcal{S}$ources

Heal, Jeanne. *You and Your Handwriting*. London: Pelham Books, 1973.

Holder, Robert. *You Can Analyze Handwriting*. Englewood Cliffs, NJ: Prentice Hall, 1958.

Marne, Patricia. *Patricia Marne's Manual of Graphology*, Ed. Peter West. Slough, England: W. Foulsham, 1999.

Roman, Klara G. *Handwriting: a Key to Personality*. New York: Pantheon Books, 1952.

Singer, Eric. *A Manual of Graphology*. London: Duckworth, 1953.

———. *Personality in Handwriting*. London: Duckworth, 1954.

Stocker, Richard Dimsdale. *The Language of Handwriting*. No. Hollywood, Calif.: Newcastle Publishing, 1994.

Index

About the Author

Paula Roberts is known internationally as the "English Psychic." In 1971 she joined the Spiritualist Association of Great Britain, where she developed her powers of intuition and clairvoyance. She is also know for her ability in ghost-hunting and her successes have been documented in leading journals of psychic research as well as many television shows.

In 1973, while still in London, Ms. Roberts studied graphology with Patricia Marne (Chair of the British Graphology Society), considered to be one of England's leading graphologists. Ms. Roberts found she had an immediate affinity with handwriting analysis and since that time has incorporated it into her psychic counseling sessions.

She always starts a session with the client's own handwriting, followed by compatibility studies of the subject's family, friends, and associates. She has also lectured frequently on handwriting analysis to groups such as psychology majors, senior citizen organizations, and graphology societies.

This long and extensive practice with people of all backgrounds and nationalities has provided her with invaluable knowledge in assessing relationships through handwriting compatibility. She also has experience in detecting the origins of poison pen letters and forgeries. It is this wealth of experience that she brings to this book.

Ms. Roberts has lived and worked in New York City since 1978.